# Advanced Java Programming



Dr.R. Anandan, B.E., M.S., Ph.D.,

Chartered Engineer, Professor, Department of CSE,

School of Engineering,

Vels Institute of Science, Technology and Advanced Studies (VISTAS),

Pallavaram, Chennai - 117.

Sreenivasulu Bolla, B.Tech., M.Tech

Assistant Professor, Department of CSE,

RISE Krishana Sai Group of Institutions,

NH-5, Valluru, ONGOLE- 523 272,

Prakasam District, Andhra Pradesh.

Published by

BONFRING®
Intellectual Integrity

**Advanced Java Programming**



9 789387 862425 >

**ISBN 978-93-87862-42-5**

**Authors**

Dr.R. Anandan

Sreenivasulu Bolla

**Bonfring**

309, 2nd Floor,

5th Street Extension,

Gandhipuram,

Coimbatore-641 012.

Tamilnadu, India.

E-mail: info@bonfring.org

Website: www.bonfring.org

Phone: 0422 4213231

# Preface

The book **"Advanced Java Programming"** is the consequence of our unyielding work. It is the versatile work that every Engineering and Computer Science students to posses. **Dr.R. Anandan**, Professor, Department of CSE, School of Engineering, VELS Institute of Science, Technology and Advanced Studies, Pallavaram, Chennai–117 and **Sreenivasulu Bolla**, Department of CSE, RISE Krishana Sai Group of Institutions. The idea of publishing the book **"Advanced Java Programming"** dawned in our minds which would be of great benefit to Engineering and Computer Science students.

Advanced Java Programming is one of the most significant areas of Computer Science that has its applications in almost every field. This book has been authored to help students to learn basic concepts and techniques in **Java Programming** with ease.

This book has been prepared as per the syllabus of most of the Indian Foreign Universities and for the courses B.E./B.Sc/BCA/M.Sc./MCA.

The book contains six units, all the units are explained vividly in a lucid manner. An attempt has been made to keep the language as simple as possible and students will definitely be able to appreciate this book.

We hope that this book will be of great help for the students to understand the subject which in turn will help them to do well in their examination.

Suggestions for further improvement of the book will be thankfully acknowledged.

***Dr.R. Anandan***

***Sreenivasulu Bolla***

# Acknowledgement

We owe our heartfelt gratitude to respected Chancellor of Vels University **Dr.Ishari K. Ganesh**, M.Com., M.B.A., B.L., Ph.D., and Dr.Aarthi Ganesh., Pro-Chancellor (Academic) for providing us with an opportunity to author this book.

A deep sense of gratitude to **Dr.A. Jothi Murugan**, Vice President (Planning and Development) of Vels Institute of Science, Technology and Advance Studies (VISTAS) for his rocksolid backing and unstinted support he has given throughout this long and ardours travail.

Our sincere thanks to **Dr.P. Swaminathan**, Vice Chancellor for motivating us to move on into the path of innovation and research and publication of books.

We wish to place on record our gratitude to **Dr.A.R. Veeramani**, Registrar for being a source of encouragement to this great endeavour of ours.

We express our gratitude to **Dr.E.N. Ganesh**, Dean, School of Engineering, Mrs.K.Kalaivani, Head, Department of CSE, School of Engineering for their support and guidance.

We would like to thank the Director, **Prof. Dr.A.V. Bhaskar Rao**, RISE Krishana Sai Group of Institutions, for giving us an opportunity.

We would like to extend special thanks to the **Principal Dr.K.V. Subramanyam**, RISE Krishana Sai Gandhi Group of Institutions, who encouraged us to complete task.

We would like to thank **HOD, P. Isaac Paul**, extended valuable support that goes a long way for academic progress.

We take this opportunity to thank our colleagues for their support and assistance. We thank profusely all those who have helped us in some way or other in bringing out this book.

We thank the publisher for his painstaking effort in bringing out this book.

Any suggestion for the improvement of the book is most welcome.

***Dr.R. Anandan***

***Sreenivasulu Bolla***

# Authors Profile

**Dr.R. Anandan** received his Under Graduate in Computer Science and Engineering from University of Madras Masters from Birla Institute of Technology and Science. Pilani and Doctoral degree in Computer Science and Engineering from BIHER, Chennai.

He is IBMS/390 Mainframe professional and he is recognized as Chartered Engineer from Institution of Engineers in India and received fellowship from Bose Science Society, India.

He is a Professor of Computer Science and Engineering at the School of Engineering, Vels Institute of Science, Technology & Advanced Studies (VISTAS), Chennai, Tamil Nadu, India which is Pioneer Institution in Engineering. He has vast experience in corporate and all levels of Academicin Computer Science and Engineering holding both Technical and Management positions his knowledge of interests not limited to Artificial intelligence Soft Computing, Machine Learning, High Performance Computing, Big data Analytics, Image Processing,3D printing and Knowledge Engineering. Under his eminent guidance8 Ph.D Research Scholars are pursuing, under his Supervision.

He associated as Member in many reputed International and National societies like International Association of Engineers (IAENG) Hong Kong, Computer Science Teacher Association (CSTA) New York, Universal Association of Computer and Electronics Engineers, USA, Association of Computer Sciences and Information Technology (IACSIT), Singapore, Institution of Engineers, India, Computer Society of India and Indian Society of Technical Education (I.S.T.E).

He serves as Editorial Board Member / Technical Committee/ Reviewer of International Journal such Arab/UK/USA journals (Springer, Thomson Reuters, SCI, Elsevier). He servers as International Committee Members towards International Conference conducted in association with Springer and Scopus.

He has published more than 65 research papers in various International Journal such in Scopus, SCI and referred journal. He received best reviewer award for the year 2018from The International Arab Journal of Information Technology (SCI Journal) under Elsevier Publication, Netherland and the reviewer of the year 2018–2019 from Energy Review Elsevier Publication, Amsterdam, Netherland. He received Appreciation award on **Teachers Day** towards publication of articles for the academic year 2018. He is the Recipient of the award Dr APJ ABDUL KALAM BEST SCIENTIST AWARD for Computer Science Engineering from BOSE Science Society, Tamil Nadu, India and Recipient of the award Distinguished Researcher in Artificial Intelligence Award by Research under Literal Access Awards, India.

**Sreenivasulu Bolla** received his B.Tech Degree in Computer Science & Engineering from J.N.T.U Kakinada, in the year 2011.Did his M.Tech Degree in Computer Science & Engineering from J.N.T.U Kakinada, in the year 2014. Presently pursuing his Ph.D in the area of "Big Data Analytics" in the Department of Computer Science& Engineering from Vels Institute of Science, Technology and Advanced Studies, Chennai. He has 6 years of Teaching Experience. He has published 5 papers in various National & International journals. He has attended 8 seminars and workshops. He got number of NPTEL online course certificates from IIT Madras .He is currently working as an Assistant Professor in the Department of Computer Science & Engineering, RISE Krishna Sai Gandhi Group of Institutions, Ongole, Prakasam District, Andhra Pradesh.

| UNIT | CONTENTS | PAGE NO |
|---|---|---|

# UNIT I

# RECAPITULATION OF XTML, XTML5 AND JAVA SWING PACKAGE

## 1.1. Introduction

HTML stands for **H**yper**t**ext **M**arkup **L**anguage, and it is the most widely used language to write Web Pages.

- **Hypertext** refers to the way in which Web pages (HTML documents) are linked together. Thus, the link available on a webpage is called Hypertext.
- As its name suggests, HTML is a **Markup Language** which means you use HTML to simply "mark-up" a text document with tags that tell a Web browser how to structure it to display.

Originally, HTML was developed with the intent of defining the structure of documents like headings, paragraphs, lists, and so forth to facilitate the sharing of scientific information between researchers.

Now, HTML is being widely used to format web pages with the help of different tags available in HTML language.

### *Basic HTML Document*

In its simplest form, following is an example of an HTML document.

### *Live Demo*

```
<!DOCTYPE html>
<html>
  <head>
    <title>This is document title</title>
  </head>
  <body>
    <h1>This is a heading</h1>
    <p>Document content goes here.....</p>
  </body>
</html>
```

## *HTML Tags*

As told earlier, HTML is a markup language and makes use of various tags to format the content. These tags are enclosed within angle braces **<Tag Name>**. Except few tags, most of the tags have their corresponding closing tags. For example, **<html>** has its closing tag **</html>** and **<body>** tag has its closing tag **</body>** tag etc.

Above example of HTML document uses the following tags.

| Sr.No | Tag & Description |
|---|---|
| 1 | **<!DOCTYPE...>** |
| | This tag defines the document type and HTML version. |
| 2 | **<html>** |
| | This tag encloses the complete HTML document and mainly comprises of document header which is represented by <head>...</head> and document body which is represented by <body>...</body> tags. |
| 3 | **<head>** |
| | This tag represents the document's header which can keep other HTML tags like<title>, <link> etc. |
| 4 | **<title>** |
| | The <title> tag is used inside the <head> tag to mention the document title. |
| 5 | **<body>** |
| | This tag represents the document's body which keeps other HTML tags like <h1>,<div>, <p> etc. |
| 6 | **<h1>** |
| | This tag represents the heading. |
| 7 | **<p>** |
| | This tag represents a paragraph. |

To learn HTML, you will need to study various tags and understand how they behave, while formatting a textual document. Learning HTML is simple as users have to learn the usage of different tags in order to format the text or images to make a beautiful webpage.

World Wide Web Consortium (W3C) recommends to use lowercase tags starting from HTML 4.

## *HTML Document Structure*

A typical HTML document will have the following structure.

```
<html>
    <head>
    Document header related tags
  </head>
    <body>
    Document body related tags
  </body>
  </html>
```

We will study all the header and body tags in subsequent chapters, but for now let's see what is document declaration tag.

The <!DOCTYPE> Declaration

The <!DOCTYPE> declaration tag is used by the web browser to understand the version of the HTML used in the document. Current version of HTML is 5 and it makes use of the following declaration.

```
<!DOCTYPE html>
```

There are many other declaration types which can be used in HTML document depending on what version of HTML is being used. We will see more details on this while discussing <!DOCTYPE...> tag along with other HTML tags.

### *Heading Tags*

Any document starts with a heading. You can use different sizes for your headings. HTML also has six levels of headings, which use the elements **<h1>, <h2>, <h3>, <h4>, <h5>,** and **<h6>**. While displaying any heading, browser adds one line before and one line after that heading.

### *Example*

```
<!DOCTYPE html>
<html>
  <head>
    <title>Heading Example</title>
  </head>
   <body>
    <h1>This is heading 1</h1>
    <h2>This is heading 2</h2>
    <h3>This is heading 3</h3>
    <h4>This is heading 4</h4>
    <h5>This is heading 5</h5>
    <h6>This is heading 6</h6>
  </body>
</html>
```

This will produce the following result.

### *Paragraph Tag*

The **<p>** tag offers a way to structure your text into different paragraphs. Each paragraph of text should go in between an opening <p> and a closing </p> tag as shown below in the example.

### *Example*

```
<!DOCTYPE html>
<html>
  <head>
    <title>Paragraph Example</title>
  </head>
  <body>
    <p>Here is a first paragraph of text.</p>
    <p>Here is a second paragraph of text.</p>
    <p>Here is a third paragraph of text.</p>
  </body>
</html>
```

This will produce the following result.

### *Line Break Tag*

Whenever you use the **<br />** element, anything following it starts from the next line. This tag is an example of an **empty**element, where you do not need opening and closing tags, as there is nothing to go in between them.

The <br /> tag has a space between the characters **br** and the forward slash. If you omit this space, older browsers will have trouble rendering the line break, while if you miss the forward slash character and just use <br> it is not valid in XHTML.

### *Example*

```
<!DOCTYPE html>
<html>
  <head>
    <title>Line Break  Example</title>
  </head>
  <body>
    <p>Hello<br />
```

```
        You delivered your assignment ontime.<br />
        Thanks<br />
        Mahnaz</p>
    </body>
</html>
```

This will produce the following result.

***Centering Content***

You can use **<center>** tag to put any content in the center of the page or any table cell.

***Example***

```
<!DOCTYPE html>
<html>
   <head>
      <title>Centring Content Example</title>
   </head>
   <body>
      <p>This text is not in the center.</p>
         <center>
         <p>This text is in the center.</p>
      </center>
   </body>
</html>
```

This will produce following result.

***Horizontal Lines***

Horizontal lines are used to visually break-up sections of a document. The **<hr>** tag creates a line from the current position in the document to the right margin and breaks the line accordingly. For example, you may want to give a line between two paragraphs as in the given example below.

***Example***

```
<!DOCTYPE html>
<html>
   <head>
      <title>Horizontal Line Example</title>
```

```
  </head>
  <body>
    <p>This is paragraph one and should be on top</p>
    <hr />
    <p>This is paragraph two and should be at bottom</p>
  </body>
</html>
```

This will produce the following result.

Again **<hr />** tag is an example of the **empty** element, where you do not need opening and closing tags, as there is nothing to go in between them.

The **<hr />** element has a space between the characters **hr** and the forward slash. If you omit this space, older browsers will have trouble rendering the horizontal line, while if you miss the forward slash character and just use **<hr>** it is not valid in XHTML

***Preserve Formatting***

Sometimes, you want your text to follow the exact format of how it is written in the HTML document. In these cases, you can use the preformatted tag **<pre>**.

Any text between the opening **<pre>** tag and the closing **</pre>** tag will preserve the formatting of the source document.

***Example***

```
<!DOCTYPE html>
<html>
  <head>
    <title>Preserve Formatting Example</title>
  </head>
  <body>
    <pre>
      function testFunction( strText ){
        alert (strText)
      }
    </pre>
  </body>
</html>
```

This will produce the following result.

Try using the same code without keeping it inside **<pre>...</pre>** tags

### *Non Breaking Spaces*

Suppose you want to use the phrase "12 Angry Men." Here, you would not want a browser to split the "12, Angry" and "Men" across two lines.

An example of this technique appears in the movie "12 Angry Men."

In cases, where you do not want the client browser to break text, you should use a non breaking space entity ** ** instead of a normal space. For example, when coding the "12 Angry Men" in a paragraph, you should use something similar to the following code –

### *Example*

```
<!DOCTYPE html>
<html>
  <head>
    <title>Nonbreaking Spaces Example</title>
   </head>
   <body>
     <p>An example of this technique appears in the movie
     "12 Angry Men."</p>
   </body>
 </html>
```

An **HTML element** is defined by a starting tag. If the element contains other content, it ends with a closing tag, where the element name is preceded by a forward slash as shown below with few tags.

| Start Tag | Content | End Tag |
|---|---|---|
| <p> | This is paragraph content. | </p> |
| <h1> | This is heading content. | </h1> |
| <div> | This is division content. | </div> |
| <br /> | | |

So here **<p>....</p>** is an HTML element, **<h1>...</h1>** is another HTML element. There are some HTML elements which don't need to be closed, such as **<img.../>**, **<hr />** and **<br />** elements. These are known as **void elements**.

HTML documents consists of a tree of these elements and they specify how HTML documents should be built, and what kind of content should be placed in what part of an HTML document.

### *HTML Tag vs. Element*

An HTML element is defined by a *starting tag*. If the element contains other content, it ends with a *closing tag*.

For example, **<p>** is starting tag of a paragraph and **</p>** is closing tag of the same paragraph but **<p>This is paragraph</p>** is a paragraph element.

### *Nested HTML Elements*

It is very much allowed to keep one HTML element inside another HTML element.

### *Example*

```
<!DOCTYPE html>
<html>
  <head>
    <title>Nested Elements Example</title>
  </head>
  <body>
    <h1>This is <i>italic</i> heading</h1>
    <p>This is <u>underlined</u> paragraph</p>
  </body>
</html>
```

This will display the following result.

We have seen few HTML tags and their usage like heading tags **<h1>, <h2>,** paragraph tag **<p>** and other tags. We used them so far in their simplest form, but most of the HTML tags can also have attributes, which are extra bits of information.

An attribute is used to define the characteristics of an HTML element and is placed inside the element's opening tag. All attributes are made up of two parts – a **name** and a **value.**

- The **name** is the property you want to set. For example, the paragraph **<p>** element in the example carries an attribute whose name is **align**, which you can use to indicate the alignment of paragraph on the page.
- The **value** is what you want the value of the property to be set and always put within quotations. The below example shows three possible values of align attribute:**left, center** and **right**.

Attribute names and attribute values are case-insensitive. However, the World Wide Web Consortium (W3C) recommends lowercase attributes/attribute values in their HTML 4 recommendation.

### *Example*

```
<!DOCTYPE html>
<html>
  <head>
    <title>Align Attribute  Example</title>
  </head>
  <body>
    <p align = "left">This is left aligned</p>
    <p align = "center">This is center aligned</p>
    <p align = "right">This is right aligned</p>
  </body>
</html>
```

This will display the following result.

### *Core Attributes*

The four core attributes that can be used on the majority of HTML elements (although not all) are.

- Id
- Title
- Class
- Style

### *The Id Attribute*

The **id** attribute of an HTML tag can be used to uniquely identify any element within an HTML page. There are two primary reasons that you might want to use an id attribute on an element.

- If an element carries an id attribute as a unique identifier, it is possible to identify just that element and its content.
- If you have two elements of the same name within a Web page (or style sheet), you can use the id attribute to distinguish between elements that have the same name.

We will discuss style sheet in separate tutorial. For now, let's use the id attribute to distinguish between two paragraph elements as shown below.

***Example***

```
<p id = "html">This para explains what is HTML</p>
<p id = "css">This para explains what is Cascading Style Sheet</p>
```

***The Title Attribute***

The **title** attribute gives a suggested title for the element. They syntax for the **title** attribute is similar as explained for **id** attribute.

The behavior of this attribute will depend upon the element that carries it, although it is often displayed as a tooltip when cursor comes over the element or while the element is loading.

***Example***

```
<!DOCTYPE html>
<html>
  <head>
    <title>The title Attribute Example</title>
  </head>
  <body>
    <h3 title = "Hello HTML!">Titled Heading Tag Example</h3>
  </body>
</html>
```

This will produce the following result.

Now try to bring your cursor over "Titled Heading Tag Example" and you will see that whatever title you used in your code is coming out as a tooltip of the cursor.

***The Class Attribute***

The **class** attribute is used to associate an element with a style sheet, and specifies the class of element. You will learn more about the use of the class attribute when you will learn Cascading Style Sheet (CSS). So for now you can avoid it.

The value of the attribute may also be a space-separated list of class names.

***For Example***

class = "className1 className2 className3"

***The Style Attribute***

The style attribute allows you to specify Cascading Style Sheet (CSS) rules within the element.

```
<!DOCTYPE html>
<html>
  <head>
    <title>The style Attribute</title>
  </head>
  <body>
    <p style = "font-family:arial; color:#FF0000;">Some text...</p>
  </body>
</html>
```

Following tags have been introduced in older versions of HTML but all the tags marked with are part of HTML-5.

| Tag | Description | Version |
|---|---|---|
| <!--...--> | Specifies a comment | |
| **<!DOCTYPE>** | Specifies the document type | |
| <**a**> | Specifies an anchor | |
| <**abbr**> | Specifies an abbreviation | |
| <**acronym**> | Specifies an acronym | |
| <**address**> | Specifies an address element | |

| | | |
|---|---|---|
| **<applet>** | Deprecated. Specifies an applet | |
| **<area>** | Specifies an area inside an image map | |
| **<article>** | Specifies an article | |
| **<aside>** | Specifies some content loosely related to the page content. If it is removed, the remaining content still makes sense | |
| **<audio>** | Specifies a sound content | |
| **<b>** | Specifies bold text | |
| **<base>** | Specifies a base URL for all the links in a page | |
| **<basefont>** | Deprecated. Specifies a base font | |
| **<bdo>** | Specifies the direction of text display | |
| **<bdi>** | Represents text that must be isolated from its surrounding for bidirectional text formatting. It allows embedding a span of text with a different, or unknown, directionality | |
| **<bgsound>** | Specifies background music | |
| **<big>** | Specifies big text | |
| **<blink>** | Specifies a text which blinks | |

| <blockquote> | Specifies a long quotation | |
|---|---|---|
| <body> | Specifies the body element | |
| <br> | Inserts a single line break | |
| <button> | Specifies a push button | |
| <canvas> | For making graphics with a script | |
| <caption> | Specifies a table caption | |
| <center> | Deprecated. Specifies centered text | |
| <cite> | Specifies a citation | |
| <code> | Specifies computer code text | |
| <col> | Specifies attributes for table columns | |
| <colgroup> | Specifies groups of table columns | |
| <comment> | Puts a comment in the document | |
| <datalist> | A list of options for input values | |
| <dd> | Specifies a definition description | |
| <del> | Specifies deleted text | |

| | | |
|---|---|---|
| **<dfn>** | Specifiesa definition term | |
| **<dialog>** | Specifiesa dialog box or window | |
| **<dir>** | Deprecated. Specifies a directory list | |
| **<div>** | Specifies a section in a document | |
| **<dl>** | Specifies a definition list | |
| **<dt>** | Specifies a definition term | |
| **<em>** | Specifies emphasized text | |
| **<embed>** | Specifiesa container for an external (non-HTML) application | |
| **<fieldset>** | Specifies a fieldset | |
| **<figcaption>** | Specifiesa caption for a <figure> element | |
| **<figure>** | Specifies self-contained content | |
| **<font>** | Deprecated. Specifies text font, size, and color | |
| **<footer>** | Specifies a footer for a document or section | |
| **<form>** | Specifies a form | |

| **<frame>** | Specifies a sub window (a frame) | |
|---|---|---|
| **<frameset>** | Specifies a set of frames | |
| **<h1> to <h6>** | Specifies header 1 to header 6 | |
| **<head>** | Specifies information about the document | |
| **<header>** | Specifies a header for a document or section | |
| **<hr>** | Specifies a horizontal rule | |
| **<html>** | Specifies an html document | |
| **<i>** | Specifies italic text | |
| **<iframe>** | Specifies an inline sub window (frame) | |
| **<ilayer>** | Specifies an inline layer | |
| **<img>** | Specifies an image | |
| **<input>** | Specifies an input field | |
| **<ins>** | Specifies inserted text | |
| **<isindex>** | Deprecated. Specifies a single-line input field | |
| **<kbd>** | Specifies keyboard text | |

| **<keygen>** | Generate key information in a form | |
|---|---|---|
| **<label>** | Specifies a label for a form control | |
| **<layer>** | Specifies a layer | |
| **<legend>** | Specifies a title in a fieldset | |
| **<li>** | Specifies a list item | |
| **<link>** | Specifies a resource reference | |
| **<main>** | Specifies the main or important content in the document. There is only oneelement in the Document | |
| **<map>** | Specifies an image map | |
| **<mark>** | Specifies a text highlighted for reference purposes, that is for its relevance in another Context | |
| **<marquee>** | Creates a scrolling-text marquee | |
| **<menu>** | Deprecated. Specifies a menu list | |
| **<menuitem>** | Specifies a command/menu item that the user can invoke from a popup menu | |
| **<meta>** | Specifies meta data of an html document which is not displayed on the page | |

| | | |
|---|---|---|
| **<meter>** | Specifies a scalar measurement within a known range (a gauge) | |
| **<multicol>** | Specifies a multicolumn text flow | |
| **<nav>** | Specifies a section that contains only navigation links | |
| **<nobr>** | No breaks allowed in the enclosed text | |
| **<noembed>** | Specifies content to be presented by browsers that do not support the <embed>tag | |
| **<noframes>** | Specifies a noframe section | |
| **<noscript>** | Specifies a noscript section | |
| **<object>** | Specifies an embedded object | |
| **<ol>** | Specifies an ordered list | |
| **<optgroup>** | Specifies an option group | |
| **<option>** | Specifies an option in a drop-down list | |
| **<output>** | Specifies the result of a calculation | |
| **<p>** | Specifies a paragraph | |
| **<param>** | Specifies a parameter for an object | |

| | | |
|---|---|---|
| **<plaintext>** | Deprecated. Render the remainder of the document as preformatted plain text | |
| **<pre>** | Specifies preformatted text | |
| **<progress>** | Specifies a completion progress of a task | |
| **<q>** | Specifies a short quotation | |
| **<rp>** | Specifies to show browsers that do not support the ruby element | |
| **<rt>** | Specifies an text ruby annotation | |
| **<ruby>** | Specifies an ruby annotation | |
| **<s>** | Deprecated. Specifies strikethrough text | |
| **<samp>** | Specifies sample computer code | |
| **<script>** | Specifies a script | |
| **<section>** | Specifies a section in a document | |
| **<select>** | Specifies a selectable list | |
| **<spacer>** | Specifies a white space | |
| **<small>** | Specifies small text | |

| **<source>** | Specifies a media resources for media elements, defined inside video or audio Elements | |
|---|---|---|
| **<span>** | Specifies a section in a document | |
| **<strike>** | Deprecated. Specifies strikethrough text | |
| **<strong>** | Specifies strong text | |
| **<style>** | Specifies a style definition | |
| **<sub>** | Specifies subscripted text | |
| **<summary>** | Specifies a summary, caption, or legend for a given <details> | |
| **<sup>** | Specifies superscripted text | |
| **<table>** | Specifies a table | |
| **<tbody>** | Specifies a table body | |
| **<td>** | Specifies a table cell | |
| **<textarea>** | Specifies a text area | |
| **<tfoot>** | Specifies a table footer | |
| **<th>** | Specifies a table heading | |

| | | |
|---|---|---|
| **<thead>** | Specifies a table header | |
| **<time>** | Specifies a date and time <details> | |
| **<title>** | Specifies the document title | |
| **<tr>** | Specifies a table row | |
| **<track>** | Specifies a text tracks used in mediaplayers | |
| **<tt>** | Specifies teletype text | |
| **<u>** | Deprecated. Specifies underlined text | |
| **<ul>** | Specifies an unordered list | |
| **<var>** | Specifies a variable | |
| **<video>** | Specifies a text tracks used in media players | |
| **<wbr>** | Indicates a potential word break point within a <nobr> section | |
| **<xmp>** | Deprecated. Specifies preformatted text | |

**Java Swing** part of Java Foundation Classes (JFC) that is *used to create window-based applications.* It is built on the top of AWT (Abstract Windowing Toolkit) API and entirely written in java.

Unlike AWT, Java Swing provides platform-independent and lightweight components.

The javax.swing package provides classes for java swing API such as JButton, JTextField, JTextArea, JRadioButton, JCheckbox, JMenu, JColorChooser etc.

### *Difference between AWT and Swing*

There are many differences between java awt and swing that are given below.

| No. | Java AWT | Java Swing |
|---|---|---|
| 1) | AWT components are **platform-dependent**. | Java swing components are **platform-independent**. |
| 2) | AWT components are **heavyweight**. | Swing components are **lightweight**. |
| 3) | AWT **doesn't support pluggable look and feel**. | Swing **supports pluggable look and feel**. |
| 4) | AWT provides **less components** than Swing. | Swing provides **more powerful components** such as tables, lists, scrollpanes, colorchooser, tabbedpane etc. |
| 5) | AWT **doesn't follows** MVC(Model View Controller) where model representsdata,view represents presentation and controller acts as an interface between model and view. | Swing **follows** MVC. |

The hierarchy of java swing API is given below.

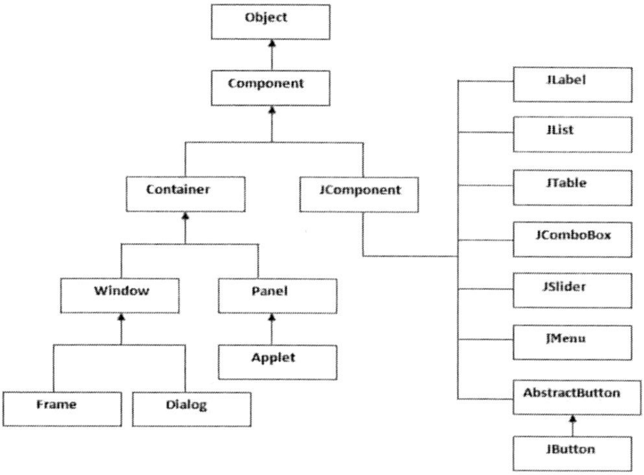


### *System Class*

The **java.lang.System** class contains several useful class fields and methods. It cannot be instantiated.Facilities provided by System.

- Standard output
- Error output streams
- Standard input and access to externally defined properties and environment variables.
- A utility method for quickly copying a portion of an array.
- A means of loading files and libraries

### *Class Declaration*

Following is the declaration for **java.lang.System** class.

```
public final class System
   extends Object Field
```

Following are the fields for **java.lang.System** class.

- **static PrintStream err** – This is the "standard" error output stream.
- **static InputStream in** – This is the "standard" input stream.
- **static PrintStream out** – This is the "standard" output stream.

### *Class Methods*

| S.N. | Method & Description |
|---|---|
| 1 | **static void arraycopy(Object src, int srcPos, Object dest, int destPos, int length)**<br>This method copies an array from the specified source array, beginning at the specified position, to the specified position of the destination array. |
| 2 | **static String clearProperty(String key)**<br>This method removes the system property indicated by the specified key. |
| 3 | **static Console console()**<br>This method returns the unique Console object associated with the current Java virtual machine, if any. |
| 4 | **static long currentTimeMillis()**<br>This method returns the current time in milliseconds. |
| 5 | **static void exit(int status)**<br>This method terminates the currently running Java Virtual Machine. |
| 6 | **static void gc()**<br>This method runs the garbage collector. |

| | |
|---|---|
| 7 | **static Map<String,String> getenv()**<br><br>This method returns an unmodifiable string map view of the current system environment. |
| 8 | **static String getenv(String name)**<br><br>This method gets the value of the specified environment variable. |
| 9 | **static Properties getProperties()**<br><br>This method determines the current system properties. |
| 10 | **static String getProperty(String key)**<br><br>This method gets the system property indicated by the specified key. |
| 11 | **static String getProperty(String key, String def)**<br><br>This method gets the system property indicated by the specified key. |
| 12 | **static SecurityManager getSecurityManager()**<br><br>This method gets the system security interface. |
| 13 | **static int identityHashCode(Object x)**<br><br>This method returns the same hash code for the given object as would be returned<br><br>by the default method hashCode(), whether or not the given object's class overrides hashCode(). |
| 14 | **static Channel inheritedChannel()**<br><br>This method returns the channel inherited from the entity that created this Java virtual machine. |
| 15 | **static void load(String filename)**<br><br>This method loads a code file with the specified filename from the local file system as a dynamic library. |
| 16 | **static void loadLibrary(String libname)**<br><br>This method loads the system library specified by the libname argument. |

| | |
|---|---|
| 17 | **static String mapLibraryName(String libname)**<br>This method maps a library name into a platform-specific string representing a native library. |
| 18 | **static long nanoTime()**<br>This method returns the current value of the most precise available system timer, in nanoseconds. |
| 19 | **static void runFinalization()**<br>This method runs the finalization methods of any objects pending finalization. |
| 20 | **static void setErr(PrintStream err)**<br>This method reassigns the "standard" error output stream. |
| 21 | **static void setIn(InputStream in)**<br>This method reassigns the "standard" input stream. |
| 22 | **static void setOut(PrintStream out)**<br>This method reassigns the "standard" output stream. |
| 23 | **static void setProperties(Properties props)**<br>This method sets the system properties to the Properties argument. |
| 24 | **static String setProperty(String key, String value)**<br>This method sets the system property indicated by the specified key. |
| 25 | **static void setSecurityManager(SecurityManager s)**<br>This method sets the System security |

### *Applet Context*

java.applet.AppletContext class provides the facility of communication between applets. We provide the name of applet through the HTML file. It provides getApplet() method that returns the object of Applet. Syntax:

```
public Applet getApplet(String name){}
```

Example of Applet Communication

```
import java.applet.*;
import java.awt.*;
import java.awt.event.*;
public class ContextApplet extends Applet implements
ActionListener{ Button b;
public void init(){
b=new Button("Click");
b.setBounds(50,50,60,50);
add(b);
b.addActionListener(this);
}
public void actionPerformed(ActionEvent e){
AppletContext ctx=getAppletContext();
Applet a=ctx.getApplet("app2");
a.setBackground(Color.yellow);
}
}
```

### *myapplet.html*

```
<html>
<body>
<applet code="ContextApplet.class" width="150" height="150"
name="app1"> </applet>
<applet code="First.class" width="150" height="150" name="app2">
</applet>
</body>
</html>
```

### *Serialization*

Java provides a mechanism, called object **serialization** where an object can be represented as a sequence of bytes that includes the object's data as well as information about the object's type and the types of data stored in the object.

After a serialized object has been written into a file, it can be read from the file and deserialized that is, the type information and bytes that represent the object and its data can be used to recreate the object in memory.

- Most impressive is that the entire process is JVM independent, meaning an object can be serialized on one platform and deserialized on an entirely different platform.
- Classes **ObjectInputStream** and **ObjectOutputStream** are high-level streams that contain the methods for serializing and deserializing an object.

The ObjectOutputStream class contains many write methods for writing various data types, but one method in particular stands out:

```
public final void writeObject(Object x) throws IOException
```

The above method serializes an Object and sends it to the output stream. Similarly, the ObjectInputStream class contains the following method for deserializing an object:

```
public final Object readObject() throws IOException, ClassNotFoundException
```

This method retrieves the next Object out of the stream and deserializes it. The return value is Object, so you will need to cast it to its appropriate data type.

To demonstrate how serialization works in Java, use the Employee class. Suppose that we have the following Employee class, which implements the Serializable interface:

```
public class Employee implements java.io.Serializable
{
   public String name;
   public String address;
   public transient int SSN;
   public int number;
    public void mailCheck()
   {
      System.out.println("Mailing a check to " + name + " " + address);
   }
}
```

Notice that for a class to be serialized successfully, two conditions must be met:

- The class must implement the java.io.Serializable interface.
- All of the fields in the class must be serializable. If a field is not serializable, it must be marked **transient**.

If you are curious to know if a Java Standard Class is serializable or not, check the documentation for the class. The test is simple: If the class implements java.io.Serializable, then it is serializable; otherwise, it's not.

### *Serializing an Object*

The **ObjectOutputStream** class is used to serialize an Object. The following SerializeDemo program instantiates an Employee object and serializes it to a file.

When the program is done executing, a file named employee.ser is created. The program does not generate any output, but study the code and try to determine what the program is doing.

**Note:** When serializing an object to a file, the standard convention in Java is to give the file a **.ser** extension.

```
import java.io.*;
public class SerializeDemo
{
   public static void main(String [] args)
   {
      Employee e = new Employee();
      e.name = "Phani Kumar";
      e.address = "Ongole";
      e.SSN = 11122333;
      e.number = 101;
      try
      {
         FileOutputStream fileOut = new
         FileOutputStream("H://employee.ser"); ObjectOutputStream out =
         new ObjectOutputStream(fileOut); out.writeObject(e);
         out.close();
         fileOut.close();
         System.out.printf("Serialized data is saved in H://employee.ser");
      }
```

```
    catch(IOException i)
    {
       i.printStackTrace();
    }
  }
}
```

***Deserializing an Object***

The following DeserializeDemo program deserializes the Employee object created in the SerializeDemo program. Study the program and try to determine its output:

```
import java.io.*;
public class DeserializeDemo
{
  public static void main(String [] args)
  {
    Employee e = null;
    try
    {
      FileInputStream fileIn = new
      FileInputStream("H://employee.ser"); ObjectInputStream in
      = new ObjectInputStream(fileIn);
      e = (Employee)
      in.readObject();
      in.close();
      fileIn.close();
    }catch(IOException i)
    {
      i.printStackTrace();
      return;
    }catch(ClassNotFoundException c)
    {
      System.out.println("Employee class not found");
```

```
        c.printStackTrace();
        return;
      }
      System.out.println("Deserialized Employee...");
      System.out.println("Name: " + e.name);
      System.out.println("Address: " + e.address);
      System.out.println("SSN: " + e.SSN);
      System.out.println("Number: " + e.number);
    }
}
```

This would produce the following result:

```
Deserialized Employee...
Name: Phani Kumar
Address:Ongole
SSN: 0
Number:101
```

Here are following important points to be noted:

- The try/catch block tries to catch a **ClassNotFoundException**, which is declared by the **readObject()** method. For a JVM to be able to deserialize an object, it must be able to find the bytecode for the class. If the JVM can't find a class during the deserialization of an object, it throws a ClassNotFoundException.
- Notice that the return value of **readObject()** is cast to an Employee reference.
- The value of the SSN field was 11122333 when the object was serialized, but because the field is **transient**, this value was not sent to the output stream. The SSN field of the deserialized Employee object is 0.

## *JAVA Collections*

Collection framework provides interfaces and class implementations that enable data handling easy and meaningful. Using collections one can store, retrieve and manipulate the data very effectively and easily.

Before we start lets first discuss the Architecture of Collection framework and hierarchy of Classes and Interfaces.

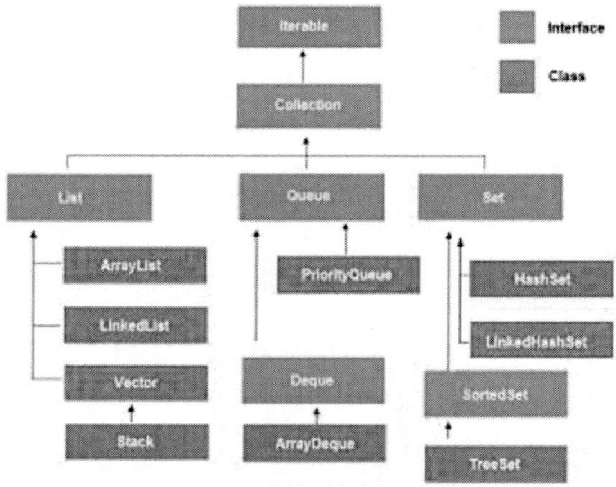


### *Collection Interface*

The Collection Interface resides at the top of the Hierarchy, although Java does not provides a direct implementation of Collection framework but Collection Interface is being implemented by List and Set Classes.

### *Data Structure*

A **data structure** is a specialized format for organizing and storing data. General data structure types include the array, the file, the record, the table, the tree, and so on. Any data structure is designed to organize data to suit a specific purpose so that it can be accessed and worked with in appropriate ways.

### *Linked List*

A **linked list** is a data structure used for collecting a sequence of objects that allows efficient addition and removal of elements in the middle of the sequence.

*Each node in a linked list is connected to the neighboring nodes.*

### *The Structure of Linked Lists*

To understand the inefficiency of arrays and the need for a more efficient data structure, imagine a program that maintains a sequence of employee names. If an employee leaves the company, the name must be removed. In an array, the hole in the sequence needs to be closed up by moving all objects that come after it. Conversely, suppose an employee is added in the middle of the sequence. Then all names following the new hire must be moved toward the end. Moving a large number of elements can involve a substantial amount of processing time.

A linked list structure avoids this movement. A linked list uses a sequence of *nodes.* A node is an object that stores an element and references to the neighboring nodes in the sequence.

A linked list consists of a number of nodes, each of which has a reference to the next node.

A Linked List Tom Diana Harry

When you insert a new node into a linked list, only the neighboring node references need to be updated.

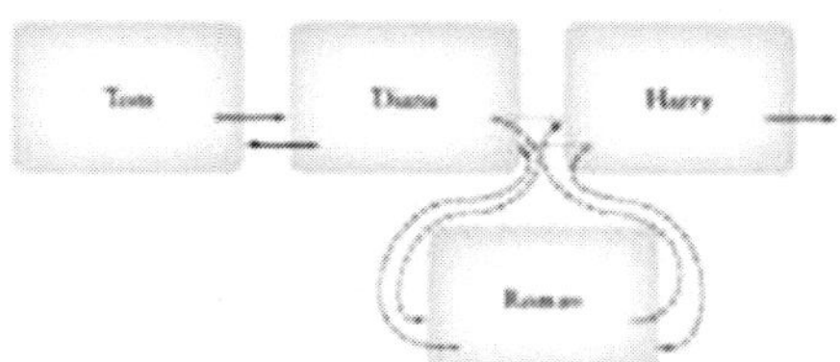

Inserting a Node into a Linked List

The same is true when you remove a node. What's the catch? Linked lists allow efficient insertion and removal, but element access can be inefficient.

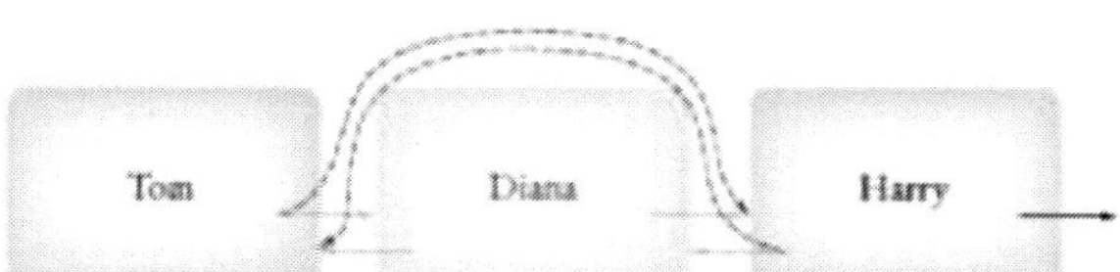


Removing a Node from a Linked List

For example, suppose you want to locate the fifth element. You must first traverse the first four. This is a problem if you need to access the elements in arbitrary order. The term "random access" is used in computer science to describe an access pattern in which elements are accessed in arbitrary (not necessarily random) order.

In contrast, sequential access visits the elements in sequence. Of course, if you mostly visit all elements in sequence (for example, to display or print the elements), the inefficiency of random access is not a problem. You use linked lists when you are concerned about the efficiency of inserting or removing elements and you rarely need element access in random order.

- The Java library provides a LinkedList class in the java.util package. It is a **generic class**, just like the ArrayList class. That is, you specify the type of the list elements in angle brackets, such as **LinkedList<String>** or **LinkedList<Employee>**.
- The below Table shows important methods of the LinkedList class. As you can see from Table, there are methods for accessing the beginning and the end of the list directly. However, to visit the other elements, you need a list **iterator**.

### *Working with Linked Lists*

| | |
|---|---|
| LinkedList<String> list = new LinkedList<String>(); | An empty list. |
| list.addLast("Harry"); | Adds an element to the end of the list. Same as add. |
| list.addFirst("Sally"); | Adds an element to the beginning of the list. list is now [Sally, Harry]. |
| list.getFirst(); | Gets the element stored at the beginning of the list; here "Sally". |
| list.getLast(); | Gets the element stored at the end of the list; here "Harry". |
| String removed = list.removeFirst(); | Removes the first element of the list and returns it. removed is "Sally" and list is [Harry]. Use removeLast to remove the last element. |

### *List Iterator*

An iterator encapsulates a position anywhere inside the linked list. Conceptually, you should think of the iterator as pointing between two elements, just as the cursor in a word processor points between two characters. In the conceptual view, think of each element as being like a letter in a word processor, and think of the iterator as being like the blinking cursor between letters.

You obtain a list iterator with the listIterator method of the LinkedList class:

**LinkedList<String> employeeNames = ...;**

**ListIterator<String> iterator = employeeNames.listIterator();**

Note that the iterator class is also a generic type. A ListIterator<String> iterates through a list of strings; a ListIterator<Book> visits the elements in a LinkedList<Book>. Initially, the iterator points before the first element.

You can move the iterator position with the next method: **iterator.next();**

The next method throws a **NoSuchElementException** if you are already past the end of the list. You should always call the iterator's **hasNext** method before calling next—it returns true if there is a next element.

```
if (iterator.hasNext())
{
   iterator.next();
}
```

The next method returns the element that the iterator is passing. When you use a **ListIterator<String>**, the return type of the next method is String. In general, the return type of the next method matches the list iterator's type parameter.

You traverse all elements in a linked list of strings with the following loop:

```
while (iterator.hasNext())
{
  String name = iterator.next();
}
```

### *Methods of the Iterator and ListIterator Interfaces*

| | |
|---|---|
| ListIterator<String> iter = list.listIterator() | Provides an iterator for visiting all list elements. |
| String s = iter.next(); | Assume that iter points to the beginning of the list [Sally] before calling next. After the call, s is "Sally" and the iterator points to the end. |
| iter.previous(); iter.set("Juliet"); | The set method updates the last element returned by next or previous. The list is now [Juliet]. |
| iter.hasNext() | Returns false because the iterator is at the end of the collection. |
| if (iter.hasPrevious()) { s = iter.previous(); } | hasPrevious returns true because the iterator is not at the beginning of the list. previous and hasPrevious are ListIterator methods. |
| iter.add("Diana"); | Adds an element before the iterator position (ListIterator only). The list is now [Diana, Juliet]. |
| iter.next(); iter.remove(); | remove removes the last element returned by next or previous. The list is now [Diana]. |

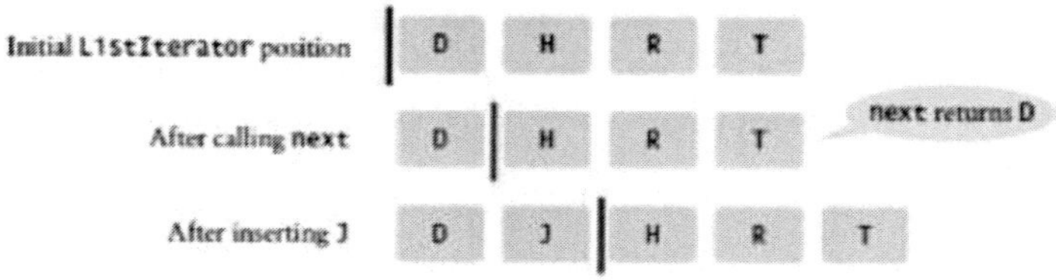


A Conceptual View of the List Iterator

***Example***

```
import java.util.LinkedList;
import java.util.ListIterator;
 /** This program demonstrates the
LinkedList class. */ public class ListDemo
{
    public static void main(String[] args)
   {
    LinkedList<String> staff = new
    LinkedList<String>(); staff.add("Diana");
    staff.add("Harry");
    staff.add("Romeo");
    staff.add("Tom");
    System.out.println("Elements are: "+staff);
    //   | in the comments indicates the iterator
    position ListIterator<String> iterator =
    staff.listIterator(); // |DHRT iterator.next(); //
    D|HRT
    iterator.next(); // DH|RT
    //Add more elements after second element
    iterator.add("Juliet"); // DHJ|RT
    iterator.add("Nina"); // DHJN|RT
    iterator.next(); // DHJNR|T
    //   Remove
    last traversed
    element
```

```
        iterator.remov
        e(); // DHJN|T
        //Print all elements
        System.out.println("After Modifications Elements are: "+staff);
    }
}
```

### *Output*

Elements are: [Diana, Harry, Romeo, Tom]

After Modifications Elements are: [Diana, Harry, Juliet, Nina, Tom]

### *Stack*

- A **stack** lets you insert and remove elements only at one end, traditionally called the *top* of the stack.
- New items can be added to the top of the stack. Items are removed from the top of the stack as well.
- Therefore, they are removed in the order that is opposite from the order in which they have been added, called ***last-in, first-out*** **or** ***LIFO*** order.

For example, if you add items A, B, and C and then remove them, you obtain C, B, and A.

With stacks, the addition and removal operations are called push and pop.

```
Stack<String> s = new Stack<String>();
s.push("A"); s.push("B"); s.push("C");
while (s.size() > 0)
{
System.out.print(s.pop() + " "); // Prints C B A
}
```

- There are many applications for stacks in computer science. Consider the undo feature of a word processor. When you select "Undo", the *last* command is undone, then the next-to-last, and so on.
- Another important example is the **run-time stack** that a processor or virtual machine keeps to store the values of variables in nested methods. Whenever a new method is called, its parameter variables and local variables are pushed onto a stack. When the method exits, they are popped off again.

- The Java library provides a simple Stack class with methods **push, pop, and peek,** the latter gets the top element of the stack but does not remove it.

***Working with Stacks***

| | |
|---|---|
| Stack<Integer> s = new Stack<Integer>(); | Constructs an empty stack. |
| s.push(1);<br>s.push(2);<br>s.push(3); | Adds to the top of the stack; s is now [1, 2, 3]. (Following the toString method of the Stack class, we show the top of the stack at the end.) |
| int top = s.pop(); | Removes the top of the stack; top is set to 3 and s is now [1, 2]. |
| head = s.peek(); | Gets the top of the stack without removing it; Head is set to 2; |

***Example***

```
import java.util.Stack;
public class StackDemo
{
    public static void main(String[] args)
    {
        Stack<String> s = new
        Stack<String>(); s.push("Phani");
        s.push("Srikanth");
        s.push("Srinu");
        System.out.println("Elements are:
        "+s);
        s.pop();
        System.out.println("After pop Elements are: ");
        while (s.size() > 0)
        {
            System.out.print(s.pop() + " ");
        }
    }
}
```

***Output***

Elements are: [Phani, Srikanth, Srinu]

After pop Elements are: Srikanth Phani

### *Queue*

A **queue** lets you add items to one end of the queue (the *tail*) and remove them from the other end of the queue (the *head*).

- Queues yield items in a *first-in, first-out* or *FIFO* fashion.
- Items are removed in the same order in which they were added.

A typical application is a print queue. A printer may be accessed by several applications, perhaps running on different computers. If each of the applications tried to access the printer at the same time, the printout would be garbled. Instead, each application places its print data into a file and adds that file to the print queue.

When the printer is done printing one file, it retrieves the next one from the queue. Therefore, print jobs are printed using the "first-in, first-out" rule, which is a fair arrangement for users of the shared printer.

- The Queue interface in the standard Java library has methods add to add an element to the tail of the queue, remove to remove the head of the queue, and peek to get the head element of the queue without removing it.

### *Working with Queues*

| | |
|---|---|
| Queue<Integer> q = new LinkedList<Integer>(); | The LinkedList class implements the Queue interface. |
| q.add(1);<br>q.add(2);<br>q.add(3); | Adds to the tail of the queue; q is now [1, 2, 3]. |
| int head = q.remove(); | Removes the head of the queue; head is set to 1 and q is [2, 3]. |
| head = q.peek(); | Gets the head of the queue without removing it; head is set to 2. |

- The LinkedList class implements the Queue interface. Whenever you need a queue, simply initialize a Queue variable with a LinkedList object:

```
Queue<String> q = new LinkedList<String>();
q.add("A"); q.add("B"); q.add("C");
while (q.size() > 0)
{
    System.out.print(q.remove() + " ");// Prints A B C
}
```

## *Set*

- The Set interface in the standard Java library has the same methods as the Collection interface.
- There is an essential difference between arbitrary collections and sets.
- A set does not admit duplicates. If you add an element to a set that is already present, the insertion is ignored.
- The Java platform contains three general-purpose Set implementations: **HashSet, TreeSet, and LinkedHashSet.**

❖ **HashSet:** which stores its elements in a hash table, is the best-performing implementation; however it makes no guarantees concerning the order of iteration.

❖ **TreeSet:** which stores its elements in a red-black tree, orders its elements based on ascending order, it is substantially slower than HashSet.

❖ **LinkedHashSet:** which is implemented as a hash table with a linked list running through it, orders its elements based on the order in which they were inserted into the set (insertion-order).

The methods declared by Set are summarized in the following table:

| SN | Methods with Description |
|---|---|
| 1 | **add( )**<br>Adds an object to the collection |
| 2 | **clear( )**<br>Removes all objects from the collection |
| 3 | **contains( )**<br>Returns true if a specified object is an element within the collection |
| 4 | **isEmpty( )**<br>Returns true if the collection has no elements |
| 5 | **iterator( )**<br>Returns an Iterator object for the collection which may be used to retrieve an object |
| 6 | **remove( )**<br>Removes a specified object from the collection |
| 7 | **size( )**<br>Returns the number of elements in the collection |

### *Example*

Set have its implementation invarious classes like HashSet, TreeSet, LinkedHashSet.

Following is the example to explain Set functionality:

```
import java.util.*;
public class SetDemo {
  public static void main(String
            args[]) {
        int count[] = {34,
        22,10,60,30,22};
    Set<Integer> set = new HashSet<Integer>();
    try{
      for(int i = 0; i<5; i++){
        set.add(count[i]);
      }
      System.out.println(set);
      TreeSet sortedSet = new TreeSet<Integer>(set);
      System.out.println("The sorted list is:");
      System.out.println(sortedSet);
      System.out.println("The First element of the set is: "+ (Integer)sortedSet.first());
      System.out.println("The last element of the set is: "+ (Integer)sortedSet.last());
    }
    catch(Exception e){}
  }
}
```

This would produce the following result:

```
[amrood]$ java SetDemo
[34, 30, 60, 10, 22]
The sorted list is:
[10, 22, 30, 34, 60]
 The First element of the set is: 10
 The last element of the set is: 60
```

### *Map Interface*

The Map interface maps unique keys to values. A key is an object that you use to retrieve a value at a later date.

- Given a key and a value, you can store the value in a Map object. After the value is stored, you can retrieve it by using its key.
- Several methods throw a **NoSuchElementException** when no items exist in the invoking map.
- A **ClassCastException** is thrown when an object is incompatible with the elements in a map.
- A **NullPointerException** is thrown if an attempt is made to use a null object and null is not allowed in the map.
- An **UnsupportedOperationException** is thrown when an attempt is made to change an unmodifiable map.

| SN | Methods with Description |
|---|---|
| 1 | **void clear( )**<br>Removes all key/value pairs from the invoking map. |
| 2 | **boolean containsKey(Object k)**<br>Returns true if the invoking map contains k as a key. Otherwise, returns false. |
| 3 | **boolean containsValue(Object v)**<br>Returns true if the map contains v as a value. Otherwise, returns false |
| 4 | **Set entrySet( )**<br>Returns a Set that contains the entries in the map. The set contains objects of type Map.Entry. This method provides a set-view of the invoking map. |
| 5 | **boolean equals(Object obj)**<br>Returns true if obj is a Map and contains the same entries. Otherwise, returns false. |
| 6 | **Object get(Object k)**<br>Returns the value associated with the key k. |
| 7 | **int hashCode( )** |

| | |
|---|---|
| | Returns the hash code for the invoking map. |
| 8 | **boolean isEmpty( )**<br>Returns true if the invoking map is empty. Otherwise, returns false. |
| 9 | **Set keySet( )**<br>Returns a Set that contains the keys in the invoking map. This method provides a set-view of the keys in the invoking map. |
| 10 | **Object put(Object k, Object v)**<br>Puts an entry in the invoking map, overwriting any previous value associated with the key. The key and value are k and v, respectively. Returns null if the key did not already exist. Otherwise, the previous value linked to the key is returned. |
| 11 | **void putAll(Map m)**<br>Puts all the entries from m into this map. |
| 12 | **Object remove(Object k)**<br>Removes the entry whose key equals k. |
| 13 | **int size( )**<br>Returns the number of key/value pairs in the map. |
| 14 | **Collection values( )**<br>Returns a collection containing the values in the map. This method provides a collection-view of the values in the map. |

### *Example*

Map has its implementation in various classes like HashMap. Following is the example to explain map functionality:

```
import java.util.*;
public class CollectionsDemo {
   public static void main(String[] args) {
      Map<String,Integer> m1 = new HashMap<String,Integer > ();
      m1.put("Zara", "8");
      m1.put("Mahnaz", "31");
      m1.put("Ayan", "12");
      m1.put("Daisy", "14");
      System.out.println();
```

```
        System.out.println(" Map Elements");
      System.out.print("\t" + m1);
   }
}
```

This would produce the following result:

Map Elements

{Mahnaz=31, Ayan=12, Daisy=14, Zara=8}

### *Generics*

Generics was added in Java 5 to provide **compile-time type checking** and removing risk of **ClassCastException** that was common while working with collection classes. The whole collection framework was re-written to use generics for type-safety. Let's see how generics help us using collection classes safely.

```
List list = new ArrayList();
list.add("abc");
list.add(new Integer(5)); //OK
String str=(String) list.get(0); //type casting leading to ClassCastException at
runtime String str=(String) list.get(1);
```

Above code compiles fine but throws **ClassCastException** at runtime because we are trying to cast Object in the list to String whereas one of the element is of type Integer. After Java 5, we use collection classes like below.

```
List<String> list1 = new ArrayList<String>();
// java 7 ? List<String> list1 = new ArrayList<>();
list1.add("abc");
//list1.add(new Integer(5)); //compiler error
for(String str : list1){
    //no type casting needed, avoids ClassCastException
}
```

Notice that at the time of list creation, we have specified that the type of elements in the list will be **String**. So if we try to add any other type of object in the list, the program will throw **compile time error**. Also notice that in for loop, we **don't need type casting** of the element in the list, hence removing the **ClassCastException** at runtime.

### *Generic Class*

We can define our own classes with generics type. A generic type is a class or interface that is parameterized over types. We use angle brackets **(< >)** to specify the **type parameter**.

To understand the benefit, let's see we have a simple class as:

```
public class GenericsTypeOld
{
        private Object t;

        public Object get()
        {
                return t;
        }
        public void set(Object t)
        {
                this.t = t;
        }
        public static void main(String args[])
        {
                GenericsTypeOld type = new GenericsTypeOld();
                type.set("Pankaj");
   String str = (String) type.get(); //type casting, error prone and can cause ClassCastException
        }
}
```

Notice that while using this class, we have to use type casting and it can produce **ClassCastException** at runtime. Now we will use java generic class to rewrite the same class as shown below.

```
public class GenericsType<T>
{
        private T t;
        public T get()
        {
                return this.t;
        }
        public void set(T t1)
```

```
	{
		this.t=t1;
	}
	public static void main(String args[])
	{
		GenericsType<String> type = new
		GenericsType<String>();
		type.set("Pankaj"); //valid
		GenericsType type1 = new
		GenericsType(); //raw type
		type1.set("Pankaj"); //valid
		type1.set(10); //valid and autoboxing support
	}
}
```

- Notice the use of GenericsType class in the main method. We don't need to **do type-casting** and we can remove **ClassCastException** at runtime.
- If we don't provide the type at the time of creation, compiler will produce a warning that "GenericsType is a raw type. References to generic type GenericsType<T> should be parameterized".
- When we don't provide type, the type becomes Object and hence it's allowing both String and Integer objects but we should always try to avoid this because we will have to use type casting while working on raw type that can produce runtime errors.

**Tip:** We can use **@SuppressWarnings("rawtypes")** annotation to suppress the compiler warning, check out java annotations tutorial.

- Also notice that it supports java **autoboxing**. That means, the numerical number is automatically convert into String.

## *Java Generic Type*

- Java Generic Type Naming convention helps us understanding code easily and having a naming convention is one of the best practices of java programming language.
- So generics also come with its own naming conventions.
- Usually type parameter names are **single, uppercase letters** to make it easily distinguishable from java variables.
- The most commonly used type parameter names are:

- E – Element (used extensively by the Java Collections Framework, for example ArrayList, Set etc.)
- K – Key (Used in Map)
- N – Number
- T – Type
- V – Value (Used in Map)
- S,U,V etc. – 2nd, 3rd, 4th types

### *Java Generic Method*

Sometimes we don't want whole class to be parameterized, in that case we can create java generics method. Since constructor is a special kind of method, we can use generics type in constructors too.

Here is a class showing example of java generic method.

```
class GenericsType<T>
{
        private T t;
        public T get()
        {
                return this.t;
        }
        public void set(T t1)
        {
                this.t=t1;
        }
}
public class GenericsMethods
{
        //Java Generic Method
        public static <T> boolean isEqual(GenericsType<T> g1, GenericsType<T> g2)
        {
                return g1.get().equals(g2.get());
        }
        public static void main(String args[])
        {
```

```
                GenericsType<String> g1 = new
                GenericsType<>(); g1.set("Pankaj");
                GenericsType<String> g2 = new
                GenericsType<>(); g2.set("Pankaj");
                boolean isequal =
                GenericsMethods.<String>isEqual(g1, g2); //above
                statement can be written simply as
                isequal = GenericsMethods.isEqual(g1, g2);
                        System.out.println(isequal);
        }
}
```

Notice the isEqual method signature showing syntax to use generics type in methods. Also notice how to use these methods in our java program. We can specify type while calling these methods or we can invoke them like a normal method. Java compiler is smart enough to determine the type of variable to be used, this facility is called as **type inference**.

# UNIT II

# JAVA BEANS

## 2.1. Introduction to Java Beans

A *Java Bean* is a software component that has been designed to be reusable in a variety of different environments.

- Java Bean components are known as **beans**.
- Beans are dynamic in that they can be changed or customized.
- There is no restriction on the capability of a Bean. It may perform a simple function, such as changing the color of text, or a complex function.
- A Bean may be visible to an end user. One example of this is a button on a graphical user interface. A Bean may also be invisible to a user. Software to decode a stream of multimedia information in real time is an example of this type of building block.
- Through the design mode of a builder tool, you use the property sheet or bean customizer to customize the bean and then save (persist) your customized beans.

## 2.2. Advantages of Java Beans

Software component architecture provides standard mechanisms to deal with software building blocks. The following list enumerates some of the specific benefits that Java technology provides for a component developer:

- A Bean obtains all the benefits of Java's "write-once, run-anywhere" paradigm.
- The properties, events, and methods of a Bean that are exposed to an application builder tool can be controlled.
- A Bean may be designed to operate correctly in different locales, which makes it useful in global markets.
- The configuration settings of a Bean can be saved in persistent storage and restored at a later time.
- A Bean may register to receive events from other objects and can generate events that are sent to other objects.

***BDK: ---- Important (Previous Question)***

The Bean Developer Kit (BDK), available from the JavaSoft site, is a simple example of a tool that enables you to create, configure, and connect a set of Beans.

There is also a set of sample Beans with their source code. Remember, the BDK is for use with versions of Java 2 prior to 1.4. For Java 2, v1.4 you must use the Bean Builder Tool.

### *Installing the BDK*

The Java 2 SDK must be installed on your machine for the BDK to work. Confirm that the SDK tools are accessible from your environment. The BDK can then be downloaded from the JavaSoft site (**http://java.sun.com**). It is packaged as one file that is a self-extracting archive. Follow the instructions to install it on your machine. The discussion that follows assumes that the BDK is installed in a directory called **bdk**. If this is not the case with your system, substitute the proper directory.

### *Starting the BDK*

To start the BDK, follow these steps:

- Change to the directory **c:\beans\beanbox**.
- Execute the batch file called **run.bat**. This causes the BDK to display the three windows shown in the bellow Figure. **ToolBox** lists all of the different Beans that have been included with the BDK. **BeanBox** provides an area to layout and connect the Beans selected from the ToolBox. **Properties** provide the ability to configure a selected Bean. You may also see a window called **Method Tracer**, but we won't be using it.

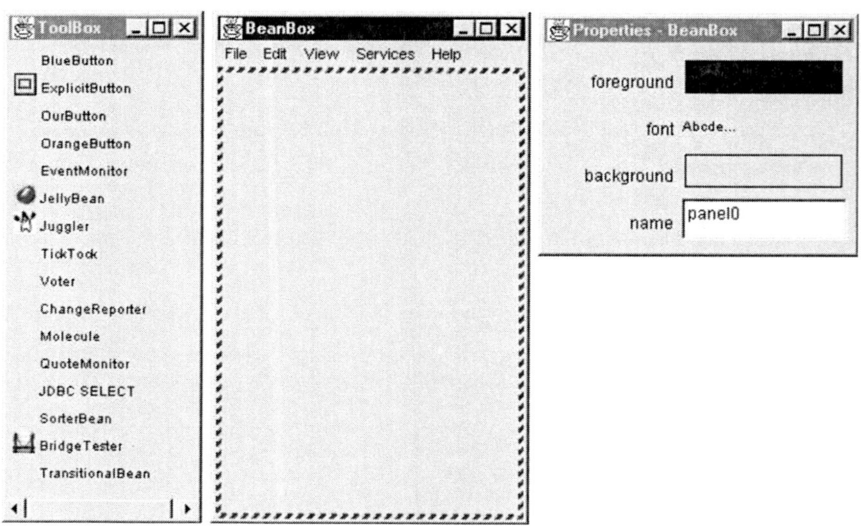


The Bean Developer Kit (BDK)

### *Using the BDK*

This section describes how to create an application by using some of the Beans provided with the BDK. First, the **Molecule** Bean displays a three-dimensional view of a molecule. It may be configured to present one of the following molecules: hyaluronic acid, benzene, buckminsterf- ullerine, cyclohexane, ethane, or water. This component also has methods that allow the molecule to be rotated in space along its X or Y axis.

Second, the **OurButton** Bean provides a push-button functionality. We will have one button labeled "Rotate X" to rotate the molecule along its X axis and another button labeled "Rotate Y" to rotate the molecule along its Y axis. The bellow Figure shows how this application appears.

### *Create and Configure an Instance of the Molecule Bean*

Follow these steps to create and configure an instance of the **Molecule** Bean:

- Positions the cursor on the ToolBox entry labeled Molecule and click the left mouse button. You should see the cursor change to a plus symbol (+).
- Move the cursor to the BeanBox display area and click the left mouse button in approximately the area where you wish the Bean to be displayed. You should see a rectangular region appear that contains a 3-D display of a molecule. This area is surrounded by a hatched border, indicating that it is currently selected.
- You can reposition the **Molecule** Bean by positioning the cursor over one of the hatched borders and dragging the Bean.
- You can change the molecule that is displayed by changing the selection in the Properties window. Notice that the Bean display changes immediately when you change the selected molecule.

### *Create and Configure an Instance of the Our Button Bean*

Follow these steps to create and configure an instance of the **OurButton** Bean and connect it to the **Molecule** Bean:

- Position the cursor on the ToolBox entry labeled **OurButton** and click the left mouse button. You should see the cursor change to a cross.
- Move the cursor to the BeanBox display area and click the left mouse button in approximately the area where you wish the Bean to be displayed. You should see a rectangular region appear that contains a button. This area is surrounded by a hatched border indicating that it is currently selected.

- You may reposition the **OurButton** Bean by positioning the cursor over one of the hatched borders and dragging the Bean.
- Go to the Properties window and change the label of the Bean to "Rotate X". The button appearance changes immediately when this property is changed.
- Go to the menu bar of the BeanBox and select Edit | Events | action | actionPerformed. You should now see a line extending from the button to the cursor. Notice that one end of the line moves as the cursor moves. However, the other end of the line remains fixed at the button.
- Move the cursor so that it is inside the **Molecule** Bean display area, and click the left mouse button. You should see the Event Target Dialog dialog box.
- The dialog box allows you to choose a method that should be invoked when this button is clicked. Select the entry labeled "rotateOnX" and click the OK button. You should see a message box appear very briefly, stating that the tool is "Generating and compiling adaptor class."

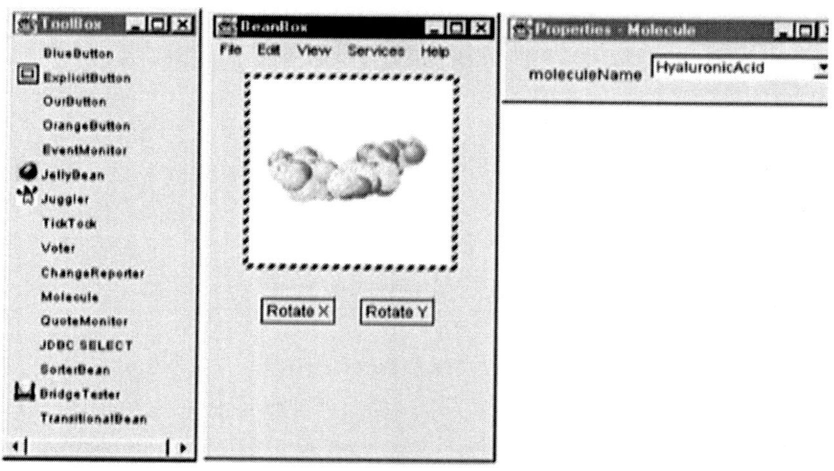


The Molecule and Our Button Beans

Test the application. Each time you press the button, the molecule should move a few degrees around one of its axes. Now create another instance of the **OurButton** Bean. Label it "Rotate Y" and map its action event to the "rotateY" method of the **Molecule** Bean. The steps to do this are very similar to those just described for the button labeled "Rotate X". Test the application by clicking these buttons and observing how the molecule moves.

## 2.3. JAR Files

Before developing your own Bean, it is necessary for you to understand JAR (Java Archive) files, because tools such as the BDK expect Beans to be packaged within JAR files. A JAR file allows you to efficiently deploy a set of classes and their associated resources.

JAR technology makes it much easier to deliver and install software. Also, the elements in a JAR file are compressed, which makes downloading a JAR file much faster than separately downloading several uncompressed files.

## 2.4. The JAR Utility

A utility is used to generate a JAR file. Its syntax is shown here:

### *jar Options Files*

The given table lists the possible options and their meanings.

| Option | Description |
|---|---|
| c | A new archive is to be created. |
| C | Change directories during command execution. |
| f | The first element in the file list is the name of the archive that is to be created or accessed. |
| m | The second element in the file list is the name of the external manifest file. |
| M | Manifest file not created. |
| t | The archive contents should be tabulated. |
| u | Update existing JAR file. |
| x | Files are to be extracted from the archive. |

The following examples show how to use this utility.

### *Creating a JAR File*

The following command creates a JAR file named **Xyz.jar** that contains all of the **.class** files in the current directory:

**jar cf Xyz.jar *.class**

If a manifest file such as **Yxz.mf** is available, it can be used with the following command:

**jar cfm Xyz.jar Yxz.mf *.class**

### *BDK Introspection ---- Important (Previous Question)*

***Introspection*** is the process of analyzing a Bean to determine its capabilities. This is an essential feature of the Java Beans API, because it allows an application builder tool to present information about a component to a software designer. Without introspection, the Java Beans technology could not operate.

- There are two ways in which the developer of a Bean can indicate which of its properties, events, and methods should be exposed by an application builder tool.
- With the first method, simple naming conventions are used. These allow the introspection mechanisms to infer information about a Bean.
- In the second way, an additional class is provided that explicitly supplies this information.

### *Design Patterns for Properties Important (Bean Properties Previous Question)*

A ***property*** is a subset of a Bean's state. The values assigned to the properties determine the behavior and appearance of that component. This section discusses **three types of properties: simple, Boolean, and indexed.**

### *Simple Properties*

A simple property has a single value. It can be identified by the following design patterns, where **N** is the name of the property and **T** is its datatype.

**public T getN( );**

**public void setN(T *arg*);**

A read/write property has both of these methods to access its values. A **read-only** property has only a **get** method. A **write-only** property has only a **set** method.

The following listing shows a class that has three read/write simple properties:

```
public class Box
{
    private double depth, height, width;
    public void setDepth(double d)
    {
            depth = d;
    }
    public double getDepth( )
    {
            return depth;
    }
    public void setHeight(double h)
    {
            height = h;
```

```
    }
    public double getHeight( )
    {
            return height;
    }
}
```

### *Boolean Properties*

A Boolean property has a value of **true** or **false**. It can be identified by the following design patterns, where **N** is the name of the property:

> **public boolean isN( );**
> **public boolean getN( );**
> **public void setN(boolean *value*);**

Either the first or second pattern can be used to retrieve the value of a Boolean property. However, if a class has both of these methods, the first pattern is used.

The following listing shows a class that has one Boolean property:

```
public class Line
{
    private boolean dotted
    =false;
    public boolean
    isDotted( )
    {
            return
    dotted;
    }
    public void setDotted(boolean dotted)
    {
            this.dotted = dotted;
    }
}
```

### *Indexed Properties*

An indexed property consists of multiple values. It can be identified by the following design patterns, where N is the name of the property and T is its datatype:

**public T getN(int *index*);**
**public void setN(int *index*, T *value*);**
**public T[ ] getN( );**
**public void setN(T *values*[ ]);**

The following listing shows a class that has one read/write indexed property:

```
public class PieChart
{
        private double data[ ];
        public double getData(int index)
        {
        return data[index];
        }
        public void setData(int index, double value)
        {
        data[index] = value;
        }
}
```

### *Design Patterns for Events ---- Important (Bean Event Previous Question)*

- Beans can generate events and send them to other objects.
- Event means any activity that interrupts the ongoing activity.
- For example when user click on mouse or press any key from the keyboard during some processing it generates an event.

These can be identified by the following design patterns, where T is the type of the event:

**public void addTListener(TListener *eventListener*);**
**public void removeTListener(TListener *eventListener*);**

These methods are used by event listeners to register an interest in events of a specific type.

- The first pattern indicates that a Bean can multicast an event to multiple listeners.
- The second pattern is used by a listener when it no longer wishes to receive a specific type of event notification from a Bean.

The following listing outlines a class that notifies other objects when a temperature value moves outside a specific range. The two methods indicated here allow other objects that implement the **TemperatureListener** interface to receive notifications when this occurs.

```
public class Thermometer
{
public void addTemperatureListener(TemperatureListener tl){
...
}
public void removeTemperatureListener(TemperatureListener tl) {
...
}
}
```

### *Methods*

- The introspection mechanism finds all of the public methods of a Bean.
- Protected and private methods are not presented.
- In a Bean component, various methods can be invoked for executing code.
- For example, Graph Bean contains a method that can invoke, there by resulting in a new data point to the graph. This code adds the value of to its internal state and hence updates the resulting display.
- In order to connect two components such as Quote Bean and Graph Bean, a mapping must be done between the event generated by the Quote Bean and the appropriate method of the Graph Bean.

### *Developing a Simple Bean Using the BDK*

This is an example that shows how to develop a simple Bean and connect it to other components via the BDK.

Our new component is called the **Colors** Bean. It appears as either a rectangle or ellipse that is filled with a color. A color is chosen at random when the Bean begins execution.

A public method can be invoked to change it. Each time the mouse is clicked on the Bean, another random color is chosen. There is one **boolean** read/write property that determines the shape. The BDK is used to lay out an application with one instance of the **Colors** Bean and one instance of the **OurButton** Bean. The button is labeled "Change." Each time it is pressed, the color changes.

### *Create a New Bean*

Here are the steps that you must follow to create a new Bean:

1. Create a directory for the new Bean.
2. Create the Java source file(s).
3. Compile the source file(s).
4. Create a manifest file.
5. Generate a JAR file.
6. Start the BDK.
7. Test.

### *Create a Directory for the New Bean*

You need to make a directory for the Bean. To follow along with this example, create *c:\beans\demo\sunw\ demo\colors*.

### *Create the Source File for the New Bean*

- The source code for the **Colors** component is shown in the following listing. It is located in the file **Colors.java**.
- The **import** statement at the beginning of the file places it in the package named **sunw.demo.colors**.
- Recall from the directory hierarchy corresponds to the package hierarchy. Therefore, this file must be located in a subdirectory named **sunw\demo\colors** relative to the **CLASSPATH** environment variable.
- The color of the component is determined by the private **Color** variable **color**, and its shape is determined by the private **boolean** variable **rectangular**.
- The constructor defines an anonymous inner class that extends **MouseAdapter** and overrides its **mousePressed( )** method.
- The **change( )** method is invoked in response to mouse presses. The component is initialized to a rectangular shape of 200 by 100 pixels.
- The **change( )** method is invoked to select a random color and repaint the component.
- The **getRectangular( )** and **setRectangular( )** methods provide access to the one property of this Bean. The **change( )** method calls **randomColor( )** to choose a color and then calls **repaint( )** to make the change visible.
- Notice that the **paint( )** method uses the **rectangular** and **color** variables to determine how to present the Bean.

```
// A simple Bean.
package sunw.demo.colors;
import java.awt.*;
import java.awt.event.*;
public class Colors extends Canvas
{
transient private Color color;
private boolean rectangular;
public Colors()
{
addMouseListener(new MouseAdapter() {
public void mousePressed(MouseEvent me) {
change();
}
});
rectangular = false;
setSize(200, 100);
change();
}
public boolean getRectangular()
{
   return rectangular;
}
public void setRectangular(boolean flag)
{
   this.rectangular = flag;
  repaint();}
  public void change()
    {
        color = randomColor();
        repaint();
    }
    private Color randomColor()
    {
```

```
        int r = (int)(255*Math.random());
        int g = (int)(255*Math.random());
        int b = (int)(255*Math.random());
        return new Color(r, g, b);
    }
    public void paint(Graphics g)
    {
        Dimension d = getSize();
        int h = d.height;
        int w = d.width;
        g.setColor(color);
        if(rectangular) {
        g.fillRect(0, 0, w-1, h-1);
    }
    else
    {
      g.fillOval(0, 0, w-1, h-1);
    }
    }
    }
```

### *Compile the Source Code for the New Bean*

Compile the source code to create a class file. Type the following:

**javac Colors.java.**

### *Create a Manifest File*

You must now create a manifest file. First, switch to the **c:\bdk\demo** directory. This is the directory in which the manifest files for the BDK demos are located. Put the source code for your manifest file in the file **colors.mft**. It is shown here:

```
Manifest-Version: 1.0
Name: sunw/demo/colors/Colors.class
Java-Bean: True
```

This file indicates that there is one **.class** file in the JAR file and that it is a Java Bean. Notice that the **Colors.class** file is in the package **sunw.demo.colors** and in the subdirectory **sunw\demo\colors** relative to the current directory.

### *Generate a JAR File*

Beans are included in the ToolBox window of the BDK only if they are in JAR files in the directory **c:\bdk\jars**. These files are generated with the jar utility. Enter the following:

**jar cfm ..\jars\colors.jar colors.mft sunw\demo\colors*.class**

This command creates the file **colors.jar** and places it in the directory **c:\bdk\jars**. (You may wish to put this in a batch file for future use.)

## 2.5. Start the BDK

Change to the directory **c:\bdk\beanbox** and type **run**. This causes the BDK to start. You should see three windows, titled ToolBox, BeanBox, and Properties. The ToolBox window should include an entry labeled "Colors" for your new Bean.

### *Create an Instance of the Colors Bean*

After you complete the preceding steps, create an instance of the **Colors** Bean in the BeanBox window. Test your new component by pressing the mouse anywhere within its borders. Its color immediately changes. Use the Properties window to change the **rectangular** property from **false** to **true**. Its shape immediately changes.

**Create and Configure an Instance of the TickTock Bean Using Bound Properties---- Important (TickTock Bean Previous question)**

A Bean that has a **bound** property generates an event when the property is changed. The event is of type **PropertyChangeEvent** and is sent to objects that previously registered an interest in receiving such notifications.

The **TickTock** Bean is supplied with the BDK. It generates a property change event every N seconds. N is a property of the Bean that can be changed via the Properties window of the BDK. The next example builds an application that uses the **TickTock** Bean to automatically control the **Colors** Bean. Figure shows how this application appears.

### *Steps*

- For this example, start the BDK and create an instance of the **Colors** Bean in the BeanBox window.
- Create an instance of the **TickTock** Bean.
- The Properties window should show one property for this component. It is "Interval" and its initial value is 5.

- This represents the number of seconds that elapse between property change events generated by the **TickTock** Bean.
- Change the value of time interval to 1.

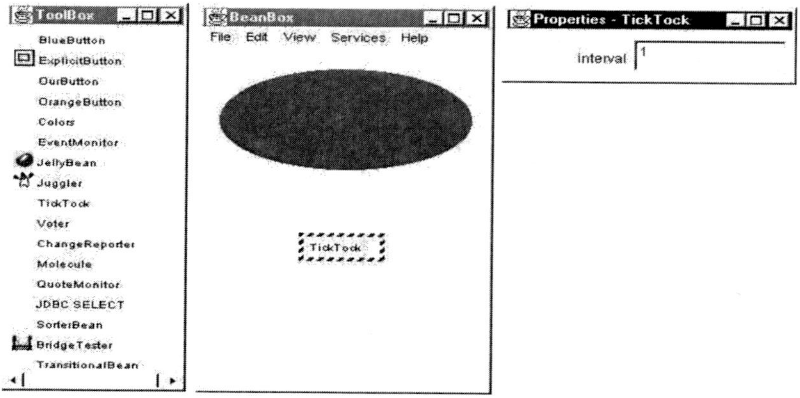


Now you need to map events generated by the **TickTock** Bean into method calls on the **Colors** Bean. Follow these steps:

- Go to the menu bar of the BeanBox and select Edit | Events | propertyChange | propertyChange. You should now see a line extending from the button to the cursor.
- Move the cursor so that it is inside the **Colors** Bean display area, and click the left mouse button. You should see the Event Target Dialog dialog box.
- The dialog box allows you to choose a method that should be invoked when this event occurs. Select the entry labeled "change" and click the OK button. You should see a message box appear very briefly, stating that the tool is "Generating and compiling adaptor class." You should now see the color of your component change every second.

```
// TickTock is an invisible bean that simply fires a property
// change event at some regular specified interval.
import java.beans.*;
import java.util.Date;
public class TickTock implements Runnable, java.io.Serializable
 {
        public TickTock()
        {
          reset();
        }
```

```
        private void reset()
        {
          runner = new Thread(this);
          runner.start();
        }
        public int getSeconds()
        {
          return (int)((new Date()).getTime()/1000);
        }
        public int getInterval()
        {
          return interval;
        }
        public void setInterval(int seconds)
        {
          interval = seconds;
          if (runner != null)
          {
            runner.interrupt();
          }
        }
    // Methods for registering listeners:
  public void addPropertyChangeListener(PropertyChangeListener l)
  {
        changes.addPropertyChangeListener(l);
  }
  public void removePropertyChangeListener(PropertyChangeListener l)
  {
        changes.removePropertyChangeListener(l);
  }
// Support for serialization
  private PropertyChangeSupport changes = new PropertyChangeSupport(this);
  private int interval = 5;
}
```

### *Using the BeanInfo Interface_---- Important (Previous Question)*

In our previous examples, design patterns were used to determine the information that was provided to a Bean user. This section describes how a developer can use the **BeanInfo** interface to explicitly control this process.

This interface defines several methods, including these:

**PropertyDescriptor[ ] getPropertyDescriptors( )**
**EventSetDescriptor[ ] getEventSetDescriptors( )**
**MethodDescriptor[ ] getMethodDescriptors( )**

They return arrays of objects that provide information about the properties, events, and methods of a Bean. By implementing these methods, a developer can designate exactly what is presented to a user. **SimpleBeanInfo** is a class that provides default implementations of the **BeanInfo** interface, including the three methods just shown. You may extend this class and override one or more of them.

The following listing shows how this is done for the **Colors** Bean that was developed earlier. **ColorsBeanInfo** is a subclass of **SimpleBeanInfo**.

It overrides **getPropertyDescriptors( )** in order to designate which properties are presented to a Bean user. This method creates a **PropertyDescriptor** object for the **rectangular** property. The **PropertyDescriptor** constructor that is used is shown here:

**PropertyDescriptor(String *property*, Class *beanCls*) throws IntrospectionException**

Here, the first argument is the name of the property, and the second argument is the class of the Bean.

```
// A Bean
information
import
sunw.demo.co
lor;
import
java.beans.*;
public class ColorsBeanInfo extends SimpleBeanInfo
{
 public PropertyDescriptor[] getPropertyDescriptors()
 {
  try
 {
   PropertyDescriptor rectangular = new PropertyDescriptor("rectangular", Colors.class);
```

```
    PropertyDescriptor pd[] = {rectangular};
    return pd;
  }
  catch(Exception e)
  {
  }
  return null;
 }
}
```

You must compile this file from the **BDK\demo** directory or set **CLASSPATH** so that it includes **c:\bdk\demo**. If you don't, the compiler won't find the **Colors.class** file properly. After this file is successfully compiled, the **colors.mft** file can be updated, as shown here:

**Name: sunw/demo/colors/ColorsBeanInfo.class**
**Name: sunw/demo/colors/Colors.class**
**Java-Bean: True**

Use the JAR tool to create a new **colors.jar** file. Restart the BDK and create an instance of the **Colors** Bean in the BeanBox. The introspection facilities are designed to look for a **BeanInfo** class. If it exists, its behavior explicitly determines the information that is presented to a Bean user. Otherwise, design patterns are used to infer this information. Bellow figure shows how the Properties window now appears. Compare it with Figure. You can see that the properties inherited from **Component** are no longer presented for the **Colors** Bean. Only the **rectangular** property appears.

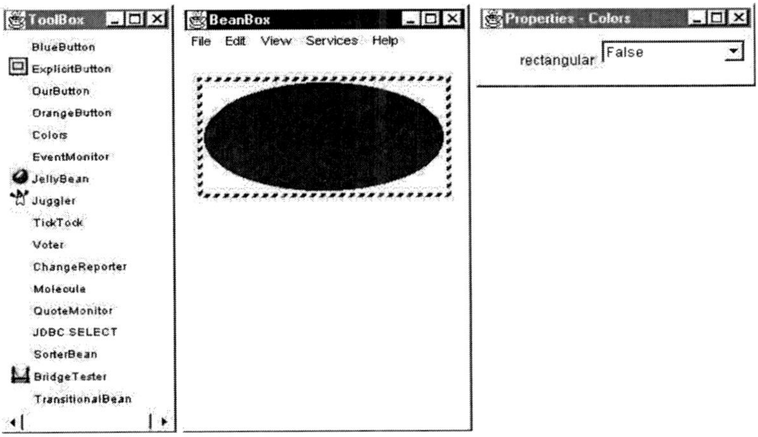

## 2.6. Constrained Properties

Constrained properties are more complicated than bound properties because they also support property change listeners which happen to be vetoers. i.e., the listeners may accept the property change or refuse it.

A Bean property is ***Constrained*** if the bean supports the java.beans. VetoableChangeListener and java.bean.propertyChangeEvent classes and the set method for this property throws a java.beans.PropertyVetoException.

The accessor methods for a constrained property are defined in the same way as those for simple properties, with the addition that the **set** method throws a PropertyVetoException. The syntax is as fallows.

```
public void setPropertyName(Type propertyName) throws PropertyVetoException
{
        Code;
}
```

The following operations in the set method must be implemented in this order:

- Save the old value in case the change is vetoed (rejected).
- Notify the listeners of the new proposed value, allowing them to veto the change.
- If no listener vetoes the change ( no exception is thrown), set the property to the new value.

## 2.7. Persistence

***Persistence*** is the ability to save a Bean to **non-volatile** storage and retrieve it at a later time. The information that is particularly important is the configuration settings.

Let us first see how the BDK allows you to save a set of Beans that have been configured and connected together to form an application. Recall our previous example involving both the **Colors** and **TickTock** Beans.

- The **rectangular** property of the **Colors** Bean was changed to **true**, and the **interval** property of the **TickTock** Bean was changed to one second.
- These changes can be saved. To save the application, go to the menu bar of the BeanBox and select File | Save. A dialog box should appear, allowing you to specify the name of a file to which the Beans and their configuration parameters should be saved. Supply a filename and click the OK button on that dialog box. Exit from the BDK.

- Start the BDK again. To restore the application, go to the menu bar of the BeanBox and select File | Load.
- A dialog box should appear, allowing you to specify the name of the file from which an application should be restored. Supply the name of the file in which the application was saved, and click the OK button. Your application should now be functioning.
- Confirm that the **rectangular** property of the **Colors** Bean is **true** and that the **interval** property for the **TickTock** Bean is equal to one second.

The object serialization capabilities provided by the Java class libraries are used to provide persistence for Beans.

If a Bean inherits directly or indirectly from **java.awt.Component**, it is automatically serializable, because that class implements the **java.io.Serializable** interface. If a Bean does not inherit an implementation of the **Serializable** interface, you must provide this yourself. Otherwise, containers cannot save the configuration of your component. The **transient and static** keywords can be used to designate data members of a Bean that should not be serialized. The **color** variable of the **Colors** class is an example of such an item.

## 2.8. Customizers

JavaBean builder tools provide support for you to create your own property editors. But often it is undesirable to have all the properties of a bean on a single property sheet. Hence Beans can be accompanied by a customize class that controls the customization of the Bean. Customizers are GUI components that contain property editors for each of the properties of the bean. Developers can write their own property editors for custom types and rely on default editors for system types. Property editors should register with an instance of the java.beans.PropertyEditorManager class.

All customizers must,

- Extend java.awt.Component or one of its subclasses.
- Implement the java.beans.Customizer interface.
- Implement a default constructor.
- Associate the customizer with its target class via BeanInfo.getBeanDescriptor.

## 2.9. The Java Beans API

The Java Beans functionality is provided by a set of classes and interfaces in the **java.beans** package. Table-1 lists the interfaces in **java.beans** and provides a brief description of their functionality. Table-2 lists the classes in **java.beans**.

| Interface Summary | |
|---|---|
| *AppletInitializer* | Methods in this interface are used to initialize Beans that are also applets. |
| *BeanInfo* | This interface allows a designer to specify information about the methods, properties, events, etc. of a bean. |
| *Customizer* | This interface allows a designer to provide a GUI through which a Bean may be configured. |
| *DesignMode* | Methods in this interface determine if a Bean is executing in design mode. |
| *PropertyChangeListener* | A "PropertyChange" event gets fired whenever a bean changes a "bound" property. |
| *PropertyEditor* | A PropertyEditor class provides support for GUIs that want to allow users to edit a property value of a given type. |
| *VetoableChangeListener* | A VetoableChange event gets fired whenever a bean changes a "constrained" property. |
| *Visibility* | Methods in this interface allow a Bean to execute in environments, where a GUI is not available. |

| Class Summary | |
|---|---|
| BeanDescriptor | A BeanDescriptor provides global information about a "bean", including its Java class, its display Name, etc. |
| Beans | This class provides some general purpose beans control methods. |
| EventSetDescriptor | An EventSetDescriptor describes a group of events that a given Java bean fires. |
| FeatureDescriptor | The FeatureDescriptor class is the common base class for PropertyDescriptor, EventSetDescriptor, and MethodDescriptor, etc. |
| IndexedPropertyDescriptor | An IndexedPropertyDescriptor describes a property that acts like an array and has an indexed read and/or indexed write method to access specific elements of the array. |
| Introspector | The Introspector class provides a standard way for tools to learn about the properties, events, and methods supported by a target Java Bean. |
| MethodDescriptor | A MethodDescriptor describes a particular method that a Java Bean supports for external access from other components. |
| ParameterDescriptor | The ParameterDescriptor class allows bean implementors to provide additional information on each of their parameters, beyond the low level type information provided by the java.lang.reflect.Method class. |
| PropertyChangeEvent | A "PropertyChange" event gets delivered whenever a bean changes a "bound" or "constrained" property. |
| PropertyChangeSupport | This is a utility class that can be used by beans that support bound properties. |
| PropertyDescriptor | A PropertyDescriptor describes one property that a Java Bean exports via a pair of accessor methods. |
| PropertyEditorManager | The PropertyEditorManager can be used to locate a property editor for any given type name. |
| PropertyEditorSupport | This is a support class to help build property editors. |
| SimpleBeanInfo | This is a support class to make it easier for people to provide BeanInfo classes. |
| VetoableChangeSupport | This is a utility class that can be used by beans that support constrained properties. |

| Exception Summary | |
|---|---|
| IntrospectionException | Thrown when an exception happens during Introspection. |
| PropertyVetoException | A PropertyVetoException is thrown when a proposed change to a property represents an unacceptable value. |

**PropertyDescriptor**, and **EventSetDescriptor** classes and the **BeanInfo** interface

```
// Show properties
andevents. package
sunw.demo.colors;
import java.awt.*;
import java.beans.*;
public class IntrospectorDemo
{
public static void main(String args[])
{
try
{
Class c = Class.forName("sunw.demo.colors.Colors");
BeanInfo beanInfo = Introspector.getBeanInfo(c);
BeanDescriptor beanDescriptor = beanInfo.getBeanDescriptor();
System.out.println("Bean name = " + beanDescriptor.getName());
System.out.println("Properties:");
PropertyDescriptor propertyDescriptor[] = beanInfo.getPropertyDescriptors();
for(int i = 0; i < propertyDescriptor.length; i++)
{
System.out.println("\t" + propertyDescriptor[i].getName());
}
System.out.println("Events:");
EventSetDescriptor eventSetDescriptor[] = beanInfo.getEventSetDescriptors();
for(int i = 0; i < eventSetDescriptor.length; i++)
{
System.out.println("\t" +
eventSetDescriptor[i].getName());
}
}
catch(Exception e)
{
System.out.println("Exception caught. " + e);
}
}}
```

The output from this program is the following:

Bean name = Colors

**Properties:**

Rectangular

**Events:**

propertyChange

component

mouseMotion mouse

hierarchy

key

focus

hierarchyBounds

inputMethod

## 2.10. EJB (Enterprise JavaBeans)

Enterprise JavaBean (EJB) technology defines a Java-based, server-side, reusable component framework for distributed applications that facilitates centrally-man-aged business logic. Let's put this definition in simple terms.

- EJBs are written in java.
- EJBs are usually executed within an applications server environment.
- EJBs can be reused.
- EJBs can be distributed across many machines and accessed almost as if they were on your local machine.
- EJBs are centrally managed by a container.

A client application wishing to interact with an enterprise bean does not have direct access to an Enterprise Bean. Rather, the bean is isolated from the client application by the EJB container, and stays under the control of it, so as to get the following services.

- Transaction management
- Persistence
- Concurrency
- Security
- Life cycle management of the bean
- Remote access to the bean
- Database connection pooling

- Events using Java Message Service (JMS)
- Deploy-time customization.

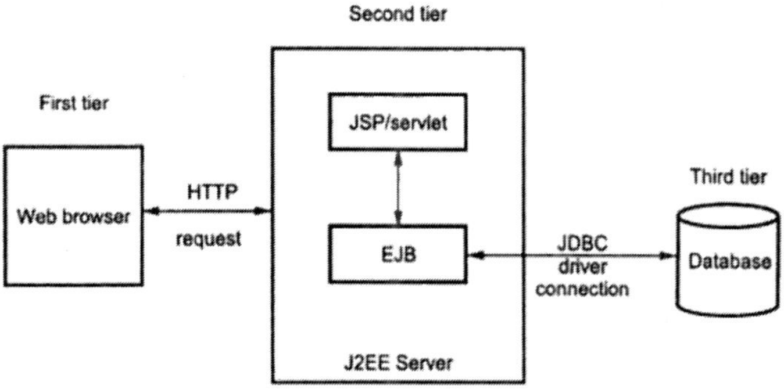


3 Tiler Architecture

EJBs are typically one part of three tier architecture as shown below:

## 2.11. Differences between JavaBean and EJBs

| JavaBean | EJB |
|---|---|
| • JavaBeans provide component architecture for applications. | • EJBs provide component architecture for distributed transaction oriented applications. |
| • JavaBeans may be visible or nonvisible at runtime. | • EJBs are nonvisible. |
| • JavaBeans are developable, configurable components. | • EJBs are developable, deployable, and configurable components. |
| • JavaBeans can be run in client side. | • EJBs can be run in server-side. |
| • JavaBeans have an external interface (BeanInfo) which allows the builder tool to interpret the functionality of the bean. | • EJBs have a deployment descriptor that describes its functionality. |
| • JavaBeans run in a JVM just like other normal java classes. | • EJBs run under the control and protection of an EJB server, and gains additional functionality, such as transaction, security, persistence, etc. |
| • JavaBeans are not typed. | • EJBs are of three types:<br>• Session<br>• Entity<br>• Message-driven |

## 2.12. Components of EJB

There are three types of EJB components.

- **Session Beans** are components implementing business logic, business rules, and workflows. For example a session Bean could perform order entry, working transaction, stock control, or database operations, session Beans tend to live for the lifetime of the client and can be used by only one client at a time.
- **Entity Beans** are components encapsulating some data contained by the enterprise. In contrast to session Beans. Entity Beans are persistent and can be shared by multiple clients.
- **MessageDriven Beans** acts as a JMS consumer, and enables asynchronous message processing. MessageDriven Beans cannot be directly called by a client as for the other EJBs. Client simply sends messages to the messaging services, and the container invokes the appropriate message Bean to consume it.

## 2.13. Important Questions

1. (a). Define BeanInfo Interface. Explain the importance of a BeanInfo Interface.

   (b). Create a simple code which utilizes the BeanInfo interface effectively.
2. Write about the following:

   (a) Bean methods

   (b) Bean properties

   (c) Bean events.
3. What is a BeanBox? Write the about BeanBox.
4. Explain the highlighting features of java bean.
5. Take the TickTock Bean available in BDK, build an application which controls the Colors Bean. Develop the necessary code to exhibit the bound properties of java beans with the above mentioned beans.
6. Explain the following given interfaces and their usage:

   i. AppletInitializer

   ii. BeanInfo

   iii. Customizer

   iv. DesignMode.
7. Explain the significance of Enterprise Java Beans in the present day 'backend business code'.

# UNIT III

# WEB SERVERS AND SERVLETS

## 3.1. Servlets

Servlets are small programs that execute on the server side of a Web connection. Just as applets dynamically extend the functionality of a Web browser, servlets dynamically extend the functionality of a Web server.

In order to understand the advantages of servlets, you must have a basic understanding of how Web browsers and servers cooperate to provide content to a user.

- Consider a request for a static Web page. A user enters a Uniform Resource Locator (URL) into a browser.
- The browser generates an HTTP request to the appropriate Web server.
- The Web server maps this request to a specific file.
- That file is returned in an HTTP response to the browser.
- The HTTP header in the response indicates the type of the content. The Multipurpose Internet Mail Extensions (MIME) are used for this purpose.
- For example, ordinary ASCII text has a MIME type of text/plain. The Hypertext Markup Language (HTML) source code of a Web page has a MIME type of text/html.

However, CGI suffered serious performance problems.

- It was expensive in terms of processor and memory resources to create a separate process for each client request.
- It was also expensive to open and close database connections for each client request.
- In addition, the CGI programs were not platform-independent.
- Therefore, other techniques were introduced. Among these are servlets.

### *Servlets Advantages*

1. Performance is significantly better. Servlets execute within the address space of a Web server. It is not necessary to create a separate process to handle each client request.
2. Servlets are platform-independent because they are written in Java. A number of Web servers from different vendors offer the Servlet API. Programs developed for this API can be moved to any of these environments without recompilation.

3. The Java security manager on the server enforces a set of restrictions to protect the resources on a server machine.
4. The full functionality of the Java class libraries is available to a servlet. It can communicate with applets, databases, or other software via the sockets and RMI mechanisms that you have seen already.

## 3.2. The Life Cycle of a Servlet

Three methods are central to the life cycle of a servlet.

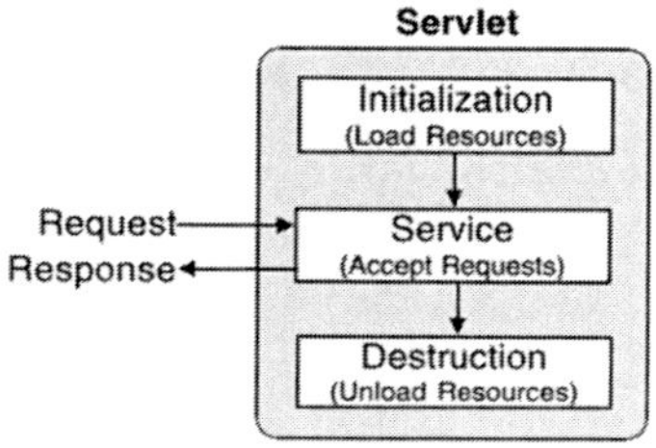


These are,

- **init( )**,
- **service( )**,
- **destroy( )**.

They are implemented by every servlet and are invoked at specific times by the server. Let us consider a typical user scenario to understand when these methods are called.

- First, assume that a user enters a Uniform Resource Locator (URL) to a Web browser. The browser then generates an HTTP request for this URL. This request is then sent to the appropriate server.
- Second, this HTTP request is received by the Web server. The server maps this request to a particular servlet. The servlet is dynamically retrieved and loaded into the address space of the server.
- Third, the server invokes the **init( )** method of the servlet. This method is invoked only when the servlet is first loaded into memory. It is possible to pass initialization parameters to the servlet so it may configure itself.
- Fourth, the server invokes the **service( )** method of the servlet. This method is called to process the HTTP request. You will see that it is possible for the servlet to read data that has been provided in the HTTP request. It may also formulate an HTTP response for the client.

- The servlet remains in the server's address space and is available to process any other HTTP requests received from clients. The service( ) method is called for each HTTP request.
- Finally, the server may decide to unload the servlet from its memory. The algorithms by which this determination is made are specific to each server. The server calls the **destroy( )** method to relinquish any resources such as file handles that are allocated for the servlet. Important data may be saved to a persistent store. The memory allocated for the servlet and its objects can then be garbage collected.

## 3.3. Tomcat For Servlet Development

To create servlets, you will need to download a servlet development environment. The one currently recommended by Sun is Tomcat 6.0, which supports the latest servlet specification.

Tomcat replaces the old JSDK (Java Servlet Development Kit) that was previously provided by Sun.

Tomcat is an open-source product maintained by the Jakarta Project of the Apache Software Foundation. It contains the class libraries, documentation, and run-time support that you will need to create and test servlets.

The examples in this chapter assume a Windows environment. The default location for Tomcat 6.0 is **C:\Program Files\Apache Tomcat 6.0** this is the location assumed by the examples you may need to set the environmental variable **JAVA_HOME** to the top-level directory in which the Java Software Development Kit is installed.

For Java 2, version 1.4, the default directory is **C:\j2sdk1.4.0**, but you will need to confirm this for your environment. To start Tomcat, select Start Tomcat in the Start | Programs menu, or run **startup.bat** from the **C:\Program Files \ Apache Tomcat 6.0\ bin** directory.

When you are done testing servlets, you can stop Tomcat by selecting Stop Tomcat in the Start | Programs menu, or run **shutdown.bat**.

The directory **C:\Program Files\Apache Tomcat 6.0\ lib** contains **Servlet-api.jar**. This JAR file contains the classes and interfaces that are needed to build servlets. To make this file accessible, update your **CLASSPATH** environment variable so that it includes **C:\Program Files\Apache Tomcat 6.0\ lib\servlet-api.jar.** Alternatively, you can specify this class file when you compile the servlets.

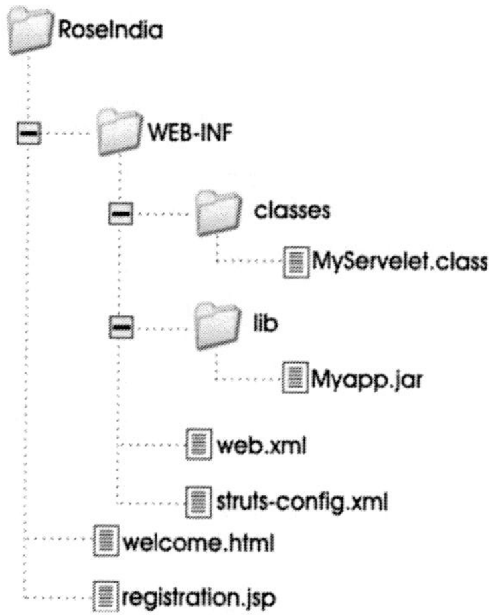


For example, the following command compiles the first servlet example:

**javac HelloServlet.java -classpath "C:\Program Files\Apache Tomcat 6.0\lib\servlet-api.jar"**

Once you have compiled a servlet, you must copy the class file into the directory that Tomcat uses for example servlet class files. For the purposes of this chapter, you must put the servlet files into the following directory:

**C:\Program Files\Apache Tomcat 6.0\webapps\RoseIndia\WEB-INF\classes.**

### *A Simple Servlet*

To become familiar with the key servlet concepts, we will begin by building and testing a simple servlet. The basic steps are the following:

1. Create and compile the servlet source code.
2. Start Tomcat.
3. Start a Web browser and request the servlet.

Let us examine each of these steps in detail.

## 3.4. Create and Compile the Servlet Source Code

To begin, create a file named **HelloServlet.java** that contains the following program:

```
import java.io.*;
import javax.servlet.*;
public class HelloServlet extends GenericServlet
```

```
{
        public void service(ServletRequest request,ServletResponse response)
        throws ServletException, IOException
        {
                response.setContentType("text/html");
                PrintWriter pw = response.getWriter();
                pw.println("<B>Hello!");
                pw.close();
        }
}
```

### *Description of the above Program*

First, note that it imports the **javax.servlet** package. This package contains the classes and interfaces required to build servlets. You will learn more about these later in this chapter. Next, the program defines **HelloServlet** as a subclass of **GenericServlet**. The **GenericServlet** class provides functionality that makes it easy to handle requests and responses.

Inside **HelloServet**, the **service( )** method (which is inherited from **GenericServlet**) is overridden. This method handles requests from a client. Notice that the first argument is a **ServletRequest** object.

This enables the servlet to read data that is provided via the client request. The second argument is a **ServletResponse** object. This enables the servlet to formulate a response for the client.

The call to **setContentType( )** establishes the MIME type of the HTTP response. In this program, the MIME type is text/html. This indicates that the browser should interpret the content as HTML source code.

### *Start a Web Browser and Request the Servlet*

Start a Web browser and enter the URL shown here:

**http://localhost:8080/examples/servlet/HelloServlet**

Alternatively, you may enter the URL shown here:

**http://127.0.0.1:8080/examples/servlet/HelloServlet**

This can be done because 127.0.0.1 is defined as the IP address of the local machine. You will observe the output of the servlet in the browser display area. It will contain the string **Hello!** in bold type.

## 3.5. The Servlet API

Two packages contain the classes and interfaces that are required to build servlets. These are:

1. **javax.servlet**
2. **javax.servlet.http**.

They constitute the Servlet API these packages are not part of the Java core packages. Instead, they are standard extensions. Therefore, they are not included in the Java Software Development Kit.

### *The javax.servlet Package*

The **javax.servlet** package contains a number of interfaces and classes that establish the framework in which servlets operate. The following table summarizes the core interfaces that are provided in this package.

The most significant of these is **Servlet.** All servlets must implement this interface or extend a class that implements the interface. The **ServletRequest** and **ServletResponse** interfaces are also very important.

| Interface | Description |
|---|---|
| Servlet | Declares life cycle methods for a servlet. |
| ServletConfig | Allows servlets to get initialization parameters. |
| ServletRequest | Used to read data from a client request. |
| ServletResponse | Used to write data to a client response. |

The following table summarizes the core classes that are provided in the **javax.servlet** package.

| Class | Description |
|---|---|
| GenericServlet | Implements the **Servlet** and **ServletConfig** interfaces. |
| ServletInputStream | Provides an input stream for reading requests from a client. |
| ServletOutputStream | Provides an output stream for writing responses to a client. |
| ServletException | Indicates a servlet error occurred. |

Let us examine these interfaces and classes in more detail.

### *The Servlet Interface*

All servlets must implement the **Servlet** interface. It declares the **init( )**, **service( )**, and **destroy( )** methods that are called by the server during the life cycle of a servlet. A method is also provided that allows a servlet to obtain any initialization parameters. The methods defined by **Servlet** are shown in Table.

| | |
|---|---|
| void destroy() | Called when the servlet is unloaded |
| String getServletInfo() | Returns a string describing the servlet |
| void init() | Called when the servlet is initialized |
| void service() | Called to process a request from a client |

The **init( )**, **service( )**, and **destroy( )** methods are the life cycle methods of the servlet. These are invoked by the server. A servlet developer overrides the **getServletInfo( )** method to provide a string with useful information (for example, author, version, date, copyright). This method is also invoked by the server.

### *The ServletConfig Interface*

The **ServletConfig** interface is implemented by the server. It allows a servlet to obtain configuration data when it is loaded. The methods declared by this interface are summarized here:

| | |
|---|---|
| getInitParameter() | Returns the value of the named servlet initialization parameter or null if no matching parameter is found. |
| getInitParameterNames() | Returns the names of all the servlet's initialization parameters as an Enumeration of String objects or an empty Enumeration if no parameters exist. |

### *The ServletRequest Interface*

The **ServletRequest** interface is implemented by the server. It enables a servlet to obtain information about a client request. Several of its methods are summarized in the Table given bellow.

| | |
|---|---|
| getAttribute() | Returns the value of the named attribute as an Object, or null if no attribute of the given name exists. |
| getAttributeNames() | Returns an Enumeration containing the names of the attributes available to this request. |
| getParameter() | Returns the value of a request parameter as a String, or null if the parameter does not exist. |
| getParameterNames() | Returns an Enumeration of String objects containing the names of the parameters contained in this request. |
| getParameterValues() | Returns an array of String objects containing all of the values the given request parameter has, or null if the parameter does not exist. |
| getContentLength() | Returns the length, in bytes, of the request body and made available by the input stream, or -1 if the length is not known. |
| getContentType() | Returns the MIME type of the body of the request, or null if the type is not known. |
| getInputStream() | Retrieves the body of the request as binary data using a ServletInputStream. |
| getLocalAddr() | Returns the Internet Protocol (IP) address of the interface on which the request was received. |
| getLocalPort() | Returns the Internet Protocol (IP) port number of the interface on which the request was received. |

### *The ServletResponse Interface*

The **ServletResponse** interface is implemented by the server. It enables a servlet to formulate a response for a client. Several of its methods are summarized in the Table given bellow.

| | |
|---|---|
| setContentType () | Sets the content type of the response being sent to the client |
| setContentLength () | Sets the length of the content body in the response |
| getOutputStream() | Returns a ServletOutputStream suitable for writing binary data in the response. |
| getWriter() | Returns a PrintWriter object that can send character text to the client. |

### *The GenericServlet Class*

The **GenericServlet** class provides implementations of the basic life cycle methods for a servlet and is typically subclassed by servlet developers. **GenericServlet** implements the **Servlet** and **ServletConfig** interfaces. In addition, a method to append a string to the server log file is available.

The signatures of this method are shown here:

**void log(String *s*)**

**void log(String *s*, Throwable *e*)**

Here, *s* is the string to be appended to the log, and *e* is an exception that occurred.

### *The ServletInputStream Class*

The **ServletInputStream** class extends **InputStream**. It is implemented by the server and provides an input stream that a servlet developer can use to read the data from a client request. It defines the default constructor. In addition, a method is provided to read bytes from the stream.

Its signature is shown here:

**int readLine(byte[ ] *buffer*, int *offset*, int *size*) throws IOException**

Reads the input stream, one line at a time. Starting at an offset, reads bytes into an array, until it reads a certain number of bytes or reaches a newline character, which it reads into the array as well.

This method returns -1 if it reaches the end of the input stream before reading the maximum number of bytes.

### *Parameters*

**buffer** - an array of bytes into which data is read

**offset** - an integer specifying the character at which this method begins reading

**size** - an integer specifying the maximum number of bytes to read

**Returns:** an integer specifying the actual number of bytes read, or -1 if the end of the stream is reached

**Throws:** java.io.IOException - if an input or output exception has occurred

### *The ServletOutputStream Class*

The **ServletOutputStream** class extends **OutputStream**. It is implemented by the server and provides an output stream that a servlet developer can use to write data to a client response. A default constructor is defined. It also defines the **print( )** and **println( )** methods, which output data to the stream.

### *The Servlet Exception Classes*

**javax.servlet** defines two exceptions. The first is **ServletException**, which indicates that a servlet problem has occurred. The second is **UnavailableException**, which extends **ServletException**. It indicates that a servlet is unavailable.

### *Reading Servlet Parameters*

The **ServletRequest** class includes methods that allow you to read the names and values of parameters that are included in a client request. We will develop a Servlet that illustrates their use.

The example contains two files:

- A Web page is defined in **PostParameters.html.**
- A servlet is defined in **PostParametersServlet.java**.
- The HTML source code for **PostParameters.html** is shown in the following listing.
- It defines a table that contains two labels and two text fields.
- One of the labels is Employee Name, Gender, and the other is Phone. There is also a submit button.
- Notice that the action parameter of the form tag specifies a URL. The URL identifies the servlet to process the HTTP POST request.

```
<html>
<body>
<center>
<form name="Form1" method="post" action="PostParametersServlet">
<table>
<tr>
<td><B>Employee</td>
<td><input type="text" name="ename" size="25" value=""></td>
</tr>
<tr>
<td><B>Phone</td>
<td><input type=textbox name="phone" size="25" value=""></td>
</tr>
<tr>
<td><B>Gender</td>
<td><input type=radio name="gender" value="male">MALE      
    <input type=radio name="gender" value="female">FEMALE </td>
</tr>
</table>
<input type=submit value="Submit">
</body>
</html>
```

The source code for **PostParametersServlet.java** is shown in the following listing. The **service( )** method is overridden to process client requests. The parameter value is obtained via the **getParameter( )** method. You can see that the parameter value is output to the client.

```
import java.io.*;
import java.util.*;
import javax.servlet.*;
public class PostParametersServlet extends GenericServlet
{
    public void service(ServletRequest request, ServletResponse response)
    throws ServletException, IOException
    {
        response.setContentType("text/html");
```

```
            PrintWriter pw = response.getWriter();

            String empname = request.getParameter("ename");
            String empphone = request.getParameter("phone");
            String empgender = request.getParameter("gender");

            pw.println("Employee Name: <b>"+empname+"</b>");
            pw.println("Employee Phone: <b>"+empphone+"</b>");
            pw.println("Employee Gender: <b>"+empgender+"</b>");
      }
}
```

Compile the servlet and perform these steps to test this example:

1. Start Tomcat (if it is not already running).
2. Display the Web page in a browser.
3. Enter an employee name and phone number in the text fields.
4. Submit the Web page.

After following these steps, the browser will display a response that is dynamically generated by the servlet.

### *The javax.servlet.http Package*

The **javax.servlet.http** package contains a number of interfaces and classes that are commonly used by servlet developers. You will see that its functionality makes it easy to build servlets that work with HTTP requests and responses.

The following table summarizes the core interfaces that are provided in this package:

| Interface | Description |
|---|---|
| HttpServletRequest | Enables servlets to read data from an HTTP request. |
| HttpServletResponse | Enables servlets to write data to an HTTP response. |
| HttpSession | Allows session data to be read and written. |

The following table summarizes the core classes that are provided in this package. The most important of these is **HttpServlet**. Servlet developers typically extend this class in order to process HTTP requests.

| Class | Description |
|---|---|
| Cookie | Allows state information to be stored on a client machine. |
| HttpServlet | Provides methods to handle HTTP requests and responses. |

### *The HttpServletRequest Interface*

The **HttpServletRequest** interface is implemented by the server. It enables a servlet to obtain information about a client request. Several of its methods are shown in the Table given bellow:

| Methods | Description |
|---|---|
| getCookies() | Returns an array containing all of the Cookie objects the client sent with this request. |
| getDateHeader() | Returns the value of the specified request header as a long value that represents a Date object. |
| getHeader() | Returns the value of the specified request header as a String. |
| getMethod() | Returns the name of the HTTP method with which this request was made, for example, GET, POST, or PUT. |
| getPathInfo() | Returns any extra path information associated with the URL the client sent when it made this request. |
| getRemoteUser() | Returns the login of the user making this request, if the user has been authenticated, or null if the user has not been authenticated. |
| getRequestedSessionId() | Returns the session ID specified by the client. |
| getRequestURL() | Reconstructs the URL the client used to make the request. |
| getServletPath() | Returns the part of this request's URL that calls the servlet. |

### *The HttpServletResponse Interface*

The **HttpServletResponse** interface is implemented by the server. It enables a Servlet to formulate an HTTP response to a client.

Several constants are defined. These correspond to the different status codes that can be assigned to an HTTP response. For example, **SC_OK** indicates that the HTTP request succeeded and **SC_NOT_FOUND** indicates that the requested resource is not available. Several methods of this interface are summarized in the given Table:

| Method | Description |
|---|---|
| addCookie() | Adds the specified cookie to the response. |
| setDateHeader() | Sets a response header with the given name and date-value |
| setHeader() | Sets a response header with the given name and value. |
| sendError(int sc) | Sends an error response to the client using the specified status code. |
| sendError(int sc, String msg) | Sends an error response to the client using the specified status. |

### *The HttpSession Interface*

The **HttpSession** interface is implemented by the server. It enables a servlet to read and write the state information that is associated with an HTTP session. Several of its methods are summarized in the given Table. All of these methods throw an **IllegalStateException** if the session has already been invalidated.

| Method | Description |
|---|---|
| getAttribute () | Returns the object bound with the specified name in this session, or null if no object is bound under the name. |
| getAttributeNames() | Returns an Enumeration of String objects containing the names of all the objects bound to this session. |
| getCreationTime() | Returns the time when this session was created, measured in milliseconds since midnight January 1, 1970 GMT |
| getId() | Returns a string containing the unique identifier assigned to this session. |
| getLastAccessedTime() | Returns the last time the client sent a request associated with this session, as the number of milliseconds since midnight January 1, 1970 GMT |

## 3.6. The Cookie Class

The **Cookie** class encapsulates a cookie. A cookie is stored on a client and contains state information. Cookies are valuable for tracking user activities. For example, assume that a user visits an online store. A cookie can save the user's name, address, and other information. The user does not need to enter this data each time he or she visits the store.

A servlet can write a cookie to a user's machine via the **addCookie( )** method of the **HttpServletResponse** interface. The data for that cookie is then included in the header of the HTTP response that is sent to the browser.

The names and values of cookies are stored on the user's machine. Some of the information that is saved for each cookie includes the following:

- The name of the cookie
- The value of the cookie
- The expiration date of the cookie
- The domain and path of the cookie

The expiration date determines when this cookie is deleted from the user's machine. If an expiration date is not explicitly assigned to a cookie, it is deleted when the current browser session ends. Otherwise, the cookie is saved in a file on the user's machine. The domain and path of the cookie determine when it is included in the header of an HTTP request. If the user enters a URL whose domain and path match these values, the cookie is then supplied to the Web server. Otherwise, it is not. There is one constructor for **Cookie**. It has the signature shown here:

Cookie(String *name*, String *value*)

Here, the name and value of the cookie are supplied as arguments to the constructor. The methods of the **Cookie** class are summarized in the given Table.

| Method | Description |
|---|---|
| String getComment( ) | Returns the comment. |
| void setComment(String *c*) | Sets the comment to *c*. |
| int getMaxAge( ) | Returns the age (in seconds). |
| void setMaxAge(int *secs*) | Sets the maximum age of the cookie to *secs*. This is the number of seconds after which the cookie is deleted. Passing –1 causes the cookie to be removed when the browser is terminated. |
| String getName( ) | Returns the name. |
| String getPath( ) | Returns the path. |
| String getValue( ) | Returns the value. |
| void setValue(String *v*) | Sets the value to *v*. |
| int getVersion( ) | Returns the cookie protocol version. (Will be 0 or 1.) |
| void setVersion(int v) | Sets the cookie protocol version to *v*, which will be 0 or 1. |

### *The HttpServlet Class*

The **HttpServlet** class extends **GenericServlet**. It is commonly used when developing servlets that receive and process HTTP requests. The methods of the **HttpServlet** class are summarized in the given Table.

### *Handling HTTP Requests and Responses*

The **HttpServlet** class provides specialized methods that handle the various types of HTTP requests. A servlet developer typically overrides one of these methods.

These methods are **doDelete( )**, **doGet( )**, **doHead( )**, **doOptions( )**, **doPost( )**, **doPut( )**, and **doTrace( )**. However, the GET and POST requests are commonly used when handling form input. Therefore, this section presents examples of these cases.

### *Handling HTTP GET Requests*

Here we will develop a servlet that handles an HTTP GET request. The servlet is invoked when a form on a Web page is submitted.

The example contains two files:

- A Web page is defined in **ColorGet.html** and a servlet is defined in **ColorGetServlet.java**.
- The HTML source code for **ColorGet.html** is shown in the following listing. It defines a form that contains a select element and a submit button.
- Notice that the action parameter of the form tag specifies a URL. The URL identifies a servlet to process the HTTP GET request.

```
<html>
<body>
<center>
<formname="Form1"
action="http://localhost:8080/examples/servlet/ColorGetServlet">
<B>Color:</B>
<select name="color" size="1">
<option value="Red">Red</option>
<option value="Green">Green</option>
<option value="Blue">Blue</option>
</select>
<br><br>
<input type=submit value="Submit">
</form>
</body>
</html>
```

- The source code for **ColorGetServlet.java** is shown in the following listing.
- The **doGet( )** method is overridden to process any HTTP GET requests that are sent to this servlet.

- It uses the **getParameter( )** method of **HttpServletRequest** to obtain the selection that was made by the user. A response is then formulated.

```
import java.io.*;
import javax.servlet.*;
import javax.servlet.http.*;
public class ColorGetServlet extends HttpServlet
{
    public void doGet(HttpServletRequest request,
    HttpServletResponse response)
    throws ServletException, IOException
    {
        String color = request.getParameter("color");
        response.setContentType("text/html");
        PrintWriter pw = response.getWriter();
        pw.println("<B>The selected color is: ");
        pw.println(color);
        pw.close();
    }
}
```

Compile the servlet and perform these steps to test this example:

1. Start Tomcat, if it is not already running.
2. Display the Web page in a browser.
3. Select a color.
4. Submit the Web page.

After completing these steps, the browser will display the response that is dynamically generated by the servlet.

**One other point:** Parameters for an HTTP GET request are included as part of the URL that is sent to the Web server. Assume that the user selects the red option and submits the form. The URL sent from the browser to the server is

**http://localhost:8080/examples/servlet/ColorGetServlet?color=Red**

The characters to the right of the question mark are known as the *query string*.

### *Handling HTTP POST Requests*

Here we will develop a servlet that handles an HTTP POST request. The servlet is invoked when a form on a Web page is submitted. The example contains two files. A Web page is defined in **ColorPost.htm** and a servlet is defined in **ColorPostServlet.java**. The HTML source code for **ColorPost.htm** is shown in the following listing. It is identical to **ColorGet.htm** except that the method parameter for the form tag explicitly specifies that the POST method should be used, and the action parameter for the form tag specifies a different servlet.

```
<html>
<body>
<center>
<form name="Form1"
method="post"
action="http://localhost:8080/examples/servlet/ColorPostServlet">
<B>Color:</B>
<select name="color" size="1">
<option value="Red">Red</option>
<option value="Green">Green</option>
<option value="Blue">Blue</option>
</select>
<br><br>
<input type=submit value="Submit">
</form>
</body>
</html>
```

The source code for **ColorPostServlet.java** is shown in the following listing. The **doPost ( )** method is overridden to process any HTTP POST requests that are sent to this servlet. It uses the **getParameter( )** method of **HttpServletRequest** to obtain the selection that was made by the user. A response is then formulated.

```
import java.io.*;
import javax.servlet.*;
import javax.servlet.http.*;
public class ColorPostServlet extends HttpServlet
{
    public void doPost(HttpServletRequest request,
```

```
        HttpServletResponse response)
        throws ServletException, IOException
        {
            String color = request.getParameter("color");
            response.setContentType("text/html");
            PrintWriter pw = response.getWriter();
            pw.println("<B>The selected color is: ");
            pw.println(color);
            pw.close();
        }
}
```

Compile the servlet and perform the same steps as described in the previous section to test it. Note: Parameters for an HTTP POST request are not included as part of the URL that is sent to the Web server. In this example, the URL sent from the browser to the server is:

**http://localhost:8080/examples/servlet/ColorGetServlet**

The parameter names and values are sent in the body of the HTTP request.

### *Using Cookies*

Now, let's develop a servlet that illustrates how to use cookies. The servlet is invoked when a form on a Web page is submitted.

The HTML source code for **login.html** is shown in the following listing. This page contains User Name and Password text fields in that values can be entered. There is also a submit button on the page. When this button is pressed, the value in the text fields are sent to **Cookies** via an HTTP POST request.

```
<html>
<body bgcolor="pink">
<form action="Cookies" method="post">
<center>User Name: <input type="test" name="user"><br>
Password:<input type="password" name="pass"><br>
<input type="submit">
<input type="Button" value="Reset">
</center>
</form>
</body>
</html>
```

The source code for **Cookies.java** is shown in the following listing. It gets the value of the parameters named "user" and "pass". It then creates a **Cookie** objects that have the names "nam1", "nam2", "nam3", "name4", "pas1", "pas2", "pas3", "pas4"and contains the values of the parameters.

```
import java.io.*;
import javax.servlet.*;
import javax.servlet.http.*;
public class login extends HttpServlet
{
    public void doPost(HttpServletRequest request, HttpServletResponse response)
      throws ServletException, IOException
      {
      response.setContentType("text/html");
       String na=request.getParameter("name");
       String pa=request.getParameter("pass");
       PrintWriter out = response.getWriter();
       Cookie nam1=new Cookie("user1","pace");
       Cookie nam2=new Cookie("user2","phani");
       Cookie nam3=new Cookie("user3","cse");
       Cookie nam4=new Cookie("user4","ece");
       Cookie pas1=new Cookie("pwd1","college");
       Cookie pas2=new Cookie("pwd2","kumar");
       Cookie pas3=new Cookie("pwd3","it");
       Cookie pas4=new Cookie("pwd4","eee");
       int flag=0;
       String nam[]={nam1.getValue(),nam2.getValue(),nam3.getValue(),nam4.getValue()};
       String pas[]={pas1.getValue(),pas2.getValue(),pas3.getValue(),pas4.getValue()};
       for(int i=0;i<4;i++)
       {
          if(nam[i].equals(na)&&pas[i].equals(pa))
          {
               flag=1;
           }
      }
```

```
            if(flag==1)
            {
             out.println("<title>The ShowMessage Servlet</title>");
                out.println("<BODY BGCOLOR=\"#FDF5E6\">\n" +"<H1 ALIGN=CENTER>
                WELCOME <br/>TO</br> " +na.toUpperCase() + "</H1>");
                out.println("</BODY></HTML>");
             }
             else
             {
                 out.println("<title>The ShowMessage Servlet</title>");
                out.println("<BODY BGCOLOR=\"#FDF5E6\">\n" + "<H1 ALIGN=CENTER> User
                is invalid </H1>");
                out.println("</BODY></HTML>");
            }
    }
}
```

Compile the servlet and perform these steps:

1. Start Tomcat, if it is not already running.
2. Display **loogin.html** in a browser.
3. Enter values for User Name and Password.
4. Submit the Web page.

After completing these steps. If the User Name and Password are matched with Cookie name and values, you will observe that the message is displayed by the browser.

Next, request the following URL via the browser:

## 3.7. Session Tracking

- HTTP is a stateless protocol.
- Each request is independent of the previous one.
- However, in some applications, it is necessary to save state information so that information can be collected from several interactions between a browser and a server.
- Sessions provide such a mechanism. A session can be created via the **getSession( )** method of **HttpServletRequest**.
- An **HttpSession** object is returned. This object can store a set of bindings that associate names with objects.

- The **setAttribute( )**, **getAttribute( )**, **getAttributeNames( )**, and **removeAttribute( )** methods of **HttpSession** manage these bindings.

The following servlet illustrates how to use session state. The **getSession( )** method gets the current session. A new session is created if one does not already exist. The **getAttribute( )** method is called to obtain the object that is bound to the name "date". That object is a **Date** object that encapsulates the date and time when this page was last accessed. (Of course, there is no such binding when the page is first accessed.) A **Date** object encapsulating the current date and time is then created. The **setAttribute( )** method is called to bind the name "date" to this object.

```
import java.io.*;
import java.util.*;
import javax.servlet.*;
import javax.servlet.http.*;
public class DateServlet extends HttpServlet
{
    public void doGet(HttpServletRequest request, HttpServletResponse response)
    throws ServletException, IOException
    {
        //Get the HttpSession object.
        HttpSession hs = request.getSession(true);
        // Get writer.
        response.setContentType("text/html");
        PrintWriter pw = response.getWriter();
        pw.print("<B>");
        // Display date/time of last access.
        Date date = (Date)hs.getAttribute("date");
        if(date != null)
        {
            pw.print("Last access: " + date + "<br>");
      }
    // Display current date/time.
    date = new Date();
```

```
        hs.setAttribute("date", date);
        pw.println("Current date: " + date);
        }
}
```

When you first request this servlet, the browser displays one line with the current date and time information. On subsequent invocations, two lines are displayed. The first line shows the date and time when the servlet was last accessed. The second line shows the current date and time.

## 3.8. Security Issues

Every servlet you put your webserver could (potentially) be exploited to damage your computer systems. All good servlet engines (such as Apache JServ or Tomcat) have high levels of security built into them; however this security is useless if your servlet is not written with security in mind.

**Example:** If we create a web interface to a database, this interface involved an applet which communicated with a servlet which communicated with a database. All of the SQL commands for connecting to the database were generated by the applet and passed to the servlet, which executed them and returned the results. The problem was that the servlet allowed any SQL command to be executed unchecked, so a malicious person could have written a new applet which sent in SQL commands to (for example) delete the entire database!

There are two possible solutions to this:-

1. Get the servlet to check the SQL and reject any malicious statements.
2. Move all the SQL into the servlet and have the applet request the relevant functions.

Method one has a serious problem, it is not fail-safe and potentially very complicated, however good your checking procedures are, there is always a risk that a malicious statement would slip through.

Method two is much safer, there is absolutely no way that a malicious user could perform any task other than the ones you have allowed, ie everything that is not specifically allowed is disallowed.

Unfortunately, there may be cases where you have to have validity checking on the submitted request, when this occurs, ensure that you rigorously test all possibilities. Try to deliberately break the security by passing requests to the servlet which would not normally be allowed by the interface and which could cause damage if they were allowed.

## 3.9. Previous Questions

1. Why doPut method is seldom used? What are the problems associated with doPut method.

**Ans: doPut():**

### *Syntax*

protected void **doPut**(HttpServletRequest req, HttpServletResponse resp) throws ServletException, java.io.IOException.

- Called by the server (via the service method) to allow a servlet to handle a PUT request.
- The PUT operation allows a client to place a file on the server and is similar to sending a file by FTP.
- When overriding this method, leave intact any content headers sent with the request (including Content-Length, Content-Type, Content-Transfer-Encoding, Content-Encoding, Content-Base, Content-Language, Content-Location, Content-MD5, and Content-Range).
- If your method cannot handle a content header, it must issue an error message (HTTP 501 - Not Implemented) and discard the request.
- This method does not either safe.
- Operations that doPut performs can have side effects for which the user can be held accountable.
- When using this method, it may be useful to save a copy of the affected URL in temporary storage.
- If the HTTP PUT request is incorrectly formatted, doPut returns an HTTP "Bad Request" message.

### *Parameters*

**req** - the HttpServletRequest object that contains the request the client made of the servlet

**resp** - the HttpServletResponse object that contains the response the servlet returns to the client.

### *Throws*

java.io.IOException - if an input or output error occurs while the servlet is handling the PUT request.

ServletException - if the request for the PUT cannot be handled.

2. Give the signature of a method which in used to read bytes from the stream for a Servlet. Explain its usage.

**Ans: The ServletInputStream Class**

- The ServletInputStream class extends InputStream.
- It is implemented by the server and provides an input stream that a servlet developer can use to read the data from a client request.
- It defines the default constructor. In addition, a method is provided to read bytes from the stream.
- Its signature is shown here:

  ***int readLine(byte[] buffer, int offset, int size) throws IOException***
- Here, *buffer* is the array into which size bytes are placed starting at *offset*.
- The method returns the actual number of bytes read or -1 if an end-of-stream condition is encountered.

*Sample example by using ServletInputStream Class are as follows:*

```
import javax.servlet.*;
import java.io.IOException;
import java.io.BufferedReader;
import java.io.PrintWriter;
public class ReadLineTestServlet extends GenericServlet
{
   public void service ( ServletRequest request, ServletResponse response ) throws
   ServletException, IOException
  {
     PrintWriter out = response.getWriter();
     ServletInputStream sins = request.getInputStream();
       int contentLen = request.getContentLength();
       if ( contentLen >= 1 )
       {
           byte buffer[] = new byte[ contentLen ];
           int len = sins.readLine( buffer, 0, buffer.length );
           String expectedResult = "ULTRA SPARC";
           //our client sent ULTRA SPARC  in the stream
           String result = new String( buffer, 0, len );
           if ( result.trim().equals( expectedResult ) )
```

```
          {
            out.println( "ReadLineTest test PASSED" );
          }
          else
           {
              out.println( "ReadLineTest test FAILED<BR>" );
              out.println( "    ServletInputStream.readLine() returned incorrect result <BR>" );
           }
        }
        else
      {
        out.println( "ReadLineTest test FAILED<BR>" );
        out.println( "    ServletRequest.getContentLength() returned incorrect result <BR>" );
      }
    }
}
```

3. Create a HTML form with three input fields first name, last name and e-mail. Pass these values to a servlet. In the servlet, verify all input fields are not null and display them back to client.

**Ans: <u>Enter.html:</u>**

```
<HTML>
 <HEAD>
        <TITLE> Servlet </TITLE>
 </HEAD>
 <BODY bgcolor="orange">
        <form action="send" method="post">
        <center>
         First Name: <input type="text" name="first">
         <br>
         Last Name: <input type="text" name="Second">
         <br>
         E-Mail: <input type="text" name="mail">
        <br>
         <input type="submit" value="Submit">
```

```
        <input type="reset">
        </center>
        </form>
 </BODY>
</HTML>
```

**Sending.java:**

```
import java.io.*;
import javax.servlet.*;
import javax.servlet.http.*;
public class Sending extends HttpServlet
{
      public void doPost(HttpServletRequest request, HttpServletResponse
response)           throws IOException, ServletException
      {
                PrintWriter pw=response.getWriter();
                response.setContentType("text/html");
                String first=request.getParameter("first");
                String last=request.getParameter("second");
                String mail=request.getParameter("mail");
                if((first!=null)&&(last!=null)&&(mail!=null))
                {
               pw.println("<html><head><title>Send Data to Servlet</title></head>");
                          pw.println("<body bgcolor='blue'><h1>");
                          pw.println("First Name: "+first+"<br>");
                          pw.println("Last Name: "+last+"<br>");
                          pw.println("Mail: "+mail+"<br>");
                }
                else
                {
                          pw.println("<html><head><title>Send Data to
Servlet</title></head>");
                          pw.println("<body bgcolor='blue'><h1>");
                          pw.println("Must enter First Name, Last Name, E-Mail");
                }
```

```
                        pw.close();
                }
        }
```

**web.xml:**

```
<web-app>
        <servlet>
                <servlet-name>send</servlet-name>
                <servlet-class>Sending</servlet-class>
        </servlet>
        <servlet-mapping>
                <servlet-name>send</servlet-name>
                <url-mapping>/sending</url-mapping>
        </servlet-mapping>
</web-app>
```

4. Develop a servlet to display time and date

   **Ans:**

```
import java.io.*;
import javax.servlet.*;
import javax.servlet.http.*;

public class datetime extends HttpServlet
{
    public void doPost(HttpServletRequest request, HttpServletResponse response)throws
IOException, ServletException
    {
            PrintWriter pw=response.getWriter();
            response.setContentType("text/html");
            Date dt=new Date();
            pw.println("<html><head><title>Display Date and Time</title></head>");
            pw.println("<body bgcolor='blue'><h1>");
            pw.println("<h1>Present date and time:"+dt+"</h1>");
    }
}
```

# UNIT IV

# JAVA SERVER PAGES

## 4.1. JSP

- JSP stands for Java Server Pages.
- JSP is part of the Java technology family, which can be used to develop dynamic web pages, which can be run on server side.
- A JSP is translated into Java servlet before being run and it processes HTTP requests and generates responses like any servlet.
- Essentially JSP pages are just normal HTML with Java codes embedded in them. So a general understanding of HTML and Java is required for learning JSP.
- Java Server Pages or JSPs, is the extended version of Java servlet technology. It combines the incorporation of the Java code and HTML for use in one single file.
- Java is known for its characteristic of "write once, run anywhere." JSP pages are platform independent.

***How JSP Works? The below is the Process***

1. The Web browser sends a request to your web server asking for a page.
2. The Web server loads the page and looks for JSP code to run.
3. If JSP code is found, the web server runs the code and sends the results to the Web browser. So the result page on the client side looks like a pure HTML page.

## 4.2. Drawbacks of Servlets

- In many Java servlet-based applications, processing the request, business logic and generating the response are handled by a single servlet class.
- Thorough Java programming knowledge is needed to develop and maintain all aspects of the application, since the processing code and the HTML elements are included together.
- Changing the presentation of the application, or changing the business logic requires the servlet code to be updated and recompile.
- After recompiled the servlet, must restart the server.
- By using web-page development tools we can't create the servlets.

## 4.3. Advantages / Benefits of JSP

JSP combines the most important features found in the alternatives:

- JSP files can easily read, write, and maintain.
- JSP supports both HTML for presentation logic and java for business logic.
- JSP pages are precompiled for efficient server processing.
- JSP pages can be used in combination with servlets that handle the business logic.
- Changing the presentation of the application, or changing the business logic, there is no need to restart the server.
- By using web-page development tools we can create the JSP's.
- JSP applications are platform independent.

***Advantages over Other Server-Side Technologies:***

***Knowledge of Java is Not a Necessity***

You do not need to learn Java, if you want to use JSP. You can use JSP technology without having any knowledge of writing Java scriplets.

***JSP Pages are Easy to Write and Easy to Maintain***

JSP is inherently easy to use, develop, support, and maintain. JSP technology has now integrated the Java Server Pages Standard Tag Library or JSTL within its fold and has also upgraded its existing functions to support the library.

***Great Speed***

The compilation of JSP pages into Java servlets takes place the first time they are called. Moreover, they are also loaded into the memory the first time itself, and then made executable for all the succeeding calls.

***Platform Independence***

JSP technology can be used on all platforms. Moreover, all its components can also run on all web servers. Moreover, JSP pages are accessible from any web servers.

## 4.4. The Anatomy/Components of a JSP Page

A JSP page is simply a regular web page with JSP elements for generating the parts of the page that differ for each request, as shown in the following figure:

**JSP code**

```
<%@ page language="java" contentType="text/html" %>        <-------- JSP element
    <html>
        <head>
            <title>Demo for Template Text</title>
        </head>
        <body bgcolor='gray'>                                <---------Template text
            <h1>Twinkle Twinkle little stars</h1>
            <h2>How I wonder what you are!!!</h2>
            <li>like a diamond in the sky</li>
            <p>

          </p>                                               <-----------Template text
          <h3>Today's Date is:

              <%= new Date().toString() %>                   <-----------------JSP element
          </h3>
      </body>                <------------------------Template text
  </html>
```

- Everything in the page that is not a JSP element is called *template text.*
- Template text can really be any text: HTML, XML, or even plain text.
- HTML is by far the most common web page language in use today, most of the descriptions and examples in this material are HTML-based, but keep in mind that JSP has no dependency on HTML; it can be used with any markup language. Template text is always passed straight through to the browser.
- When a JSP page request is processed, the template text and the dynamic content generated by the JSP elements are merged, and the result is sent as the response to the browser.

## 4.5. JSP Elements

There are three types of elements with JavaServer Pages:

1. *Directive elements*
2. *Action elements*
3. *Scripting* elements
    i. *Declarations*
    ii. Scriptlets
    iii. Expressions

### Directive Elements

The directive elements are used to specify information about the page itself that remains the same between page requests.

### Directive Elements

| Element | | Description |
|---|---|---|
| <%@ page ... %> | → | Defines page-dependent attributes, such as scripting language, error page, and buffering requirements |
| <%@ include ... %> | → | Includes a file during the translation phase |
| <%@ taglib ... %> | → | Declares a tag library, containing custom actions, used in the page |

### Action Elements

Action elements typically perform some action based on information that is required at the exact time the JSP page is requested by a client. An action element can, for instance, access parameters sent with the request to do a database lookup. It can also dynamically generate HTML, such as a table filled with information retrieved from an external system.

### Standard Action Elements

| Element | Description |
|---|---|
| <jsp:useBean> | Makes a JavaBeans component available in a page |
| <jsp:getProperty> | Gets a property value from a JavaBeans component and adds it to the response |
| <jsp:setProperty> | Sets a JavaBeans property value |
| <jsp:include> | Includes the response from a servlet or JSP page during the request processing phase |
| <jsp:forward> | Forwards the processing of a request to a servlet or JSP page |
| <jsp:param> | Adds a parameter value to a request handed off to another servlet or JSP page using <jsp:include> or <jsp:forward> |
| <jsp:plugin> | Generates HTML that contains the appropriate client browser-dependent elements (OBJECT or EMBED) needed to execute an Applet with the Java Plugin software |

### Scripting Elements

Scripting elements allow you to add small pieces of java code into a JSP page, such as an if statement to generate different HTML depending on a certain condition.

You should use scripting elements with extreme care: if you embed too much code in your JSP pages, you will end up with the same kind of maintenance problems as with servlets embedding HTML.

These are 4 types.

1. Declarations
2. Scriptlets
3. Expressions
4. Comments

### 1. *Declarations*

Used to declare instance variables and methods in the JSP page implementation class. When tomcat generates the jsp(servlet) these are inserted into the body of the servlet

Syntax of the declarations elements is:

```
<%!    Code    %>
```

As the name declaring would suggest, the same used for declaring an 'instance variable'

***Example***

```
<%!    String x;                   %>
<%!    String x = new String("hello");  %>
```

### 2. *Scriptlets*

Used to embed scripting code. When tomcat generates the jsp(servlets) these are inserted into the method _jspService()

Syntax of the Scriptlets elements is:

```
<%    Code;   %>
```

A scriptlet must be a complete java statement, meaning it ends with semicolon;

***Example***

```
<%    String x;          %>
<%x = x + "from  jspLand";     %>
```

### 3. *Expressions*

Used to embed Java expressions when the result shall be added to the response. Also used as runtime action attribute values. These are evaluated and inserted into the output of the servlet. These are commonly used to insert dynamic content into a parameter of an HTML tag.

Syntax of the Expression elements is:

**<%= Code %>**

Expression is not a complete java statement, meaning it could not ends with semicolon

***Example***

**<% = x %>**

### *4. Comments*

You can use two types of comments within a JSP. The first comment style, known as an output comment, enables the comment to appear in the output stream on the browser. This comment is an HTML formatted comment whose syntax is:

**<!-- comments ... -->**

The second comment style is used to fully exclude the commented block from the output and the commented block is never delivered to the browser. The syntax is:

**<%-- comment text --%>**

## 4.6. JSP Processing

- A JSP page cannot be sent as-is to the browser; all JSP elements must first be processed by the server. This is done by converting the JSP page into a servlet, and then compiles the servlet.
- The JSP container is often implemented as a servlet configured to handle all requests for JSP pages. In fact, these two containers - a servlet container and a JSP container - are often combined into one package under the name *web container.*
- A JSP container is responsible for converting the JSP page into a servlet (.java file ) and compiling the servlet. These two steps form the *translation phase.*
- The JSP container is also responsible for invoking the JSP page implementation class to process each request and generate the response. This is called the *request processing phase.*

A JSP page is handled exactly like a regular servlet: it's loaded once and called repeatedly, until the server is shut down.

## 4.7. JSP Life Cycle

Life cycle of a JSP page consists of two phases, translation phase and execution phase. Every JSP is a Servlet, a JSP page is translated and compiled into servlet and the resulting servlet handles the request, So life cycle of a JSP page largely depends on the Servlet API.

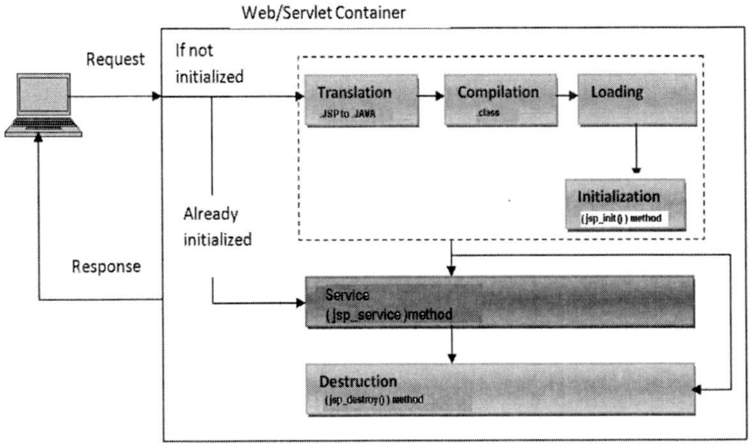


JSP engine does the following 7 phases.

- Page translation: page is parsed, and a java file which is a servlet is created.
- Page compilation: page is compiled into a class file
- Page loading: This class file is loaded.
- Create an instance: Instance of servlet is created
- jspInit() method is called
- jspService is called to handle service calls
- jspDestroy is called to destroy it when the servlet is not required.

### *Translation Phase*

During the translation phase, JSP page is translated into a servlet (.java). The entire static markup in the JSP page is converted into the code that writes the data to response stream.

If you have following HTML code into your JSP page:

**JSP life cycle tutorial**

It will generate code like:

**out.println("JSP life cycle tutorial")**

### *JSP Page Compilation*

The generated java servlet file is compiled into a java servlet class. Note: The translation of a JSP source page into its implementation class can happen at any time between initial deployment of the JSP page into the JSP container and the receipt and processing of a client request for the target JSP page.

### *Class Loading*

The java servlet class that was compiled from the JSP source is loaded into the container

### *Execution Phase*

JSP life cycle's execution phase is almost similar to that of the Servlet life cycle, because ultimately it's a servlet which is being executed. The Servlet class generated at the end of the translation phase represents the contract between container and the JSP page. According to the JSP specification the servlet class must implement the HttpJspPage interface which defines the life cycle methods. JSP life cycle includes three methods **jspInit(), _jspService() and jspDestroy().**

### *Initialization*

jspInit() method is called immediately after the instance was created. It is called only once during JSP life cycle.

### *_jspService() execution*

This method is called for every request of this JSP during its life cycle. This is where it serves the purpose of creation. It passes the request and the response objects. _jspService() cannot be overridden.

### *jspDestroy() execution*

This method is called when this JSP is destroyed. With this call the servlet serves its purpose and submits itself to heaven (garbage collection). This is the end of jsp life cycle.
jspInit(), _jspService() and jspDestroy() are called the life cycle methods of the JSP.

### *Examples*

**Program1.jsp**

**Display the current date and time.**

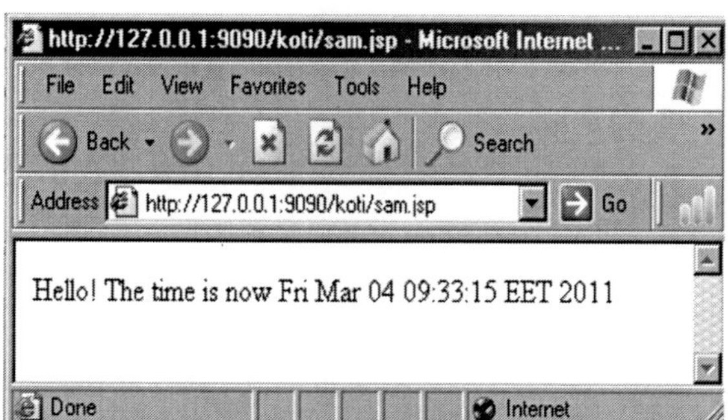

```
<HTML>
  <BODY>
     Hello!  The time is now <%= new java.util.Date () %>
  </BODY>
</HTML>
```

**Program2.jsp**

**Display the current date and time.**

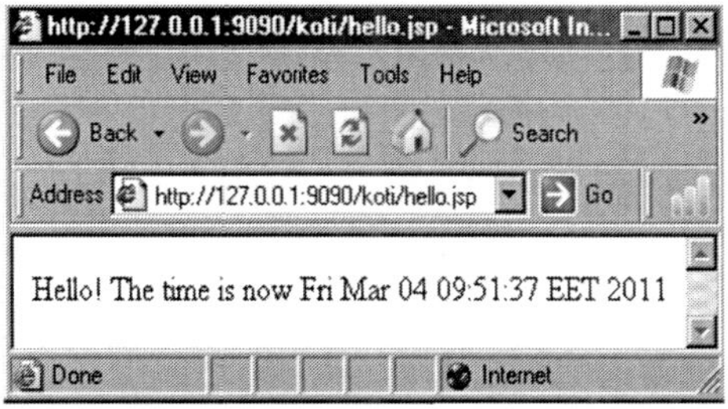


```
<%@ page import="java.util.*" %>
<HTML>
  <BODY>
      <%
        out.println( "Evaluating date now" );
         Date date = new Date();
      %>
      Hello!  The time is now <%= date %>
  </BODY>
</HTML>
```

**Program3.jsp**

**Display the time, date, and local host address**

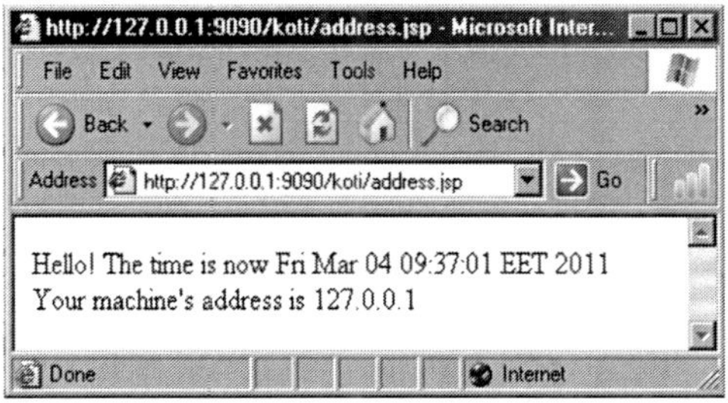

```
<HTML>
  <BODY>
      <%
        // This scriptlet declares and initializes "date"
        out.println( "Evaluating date now" );
        java.util.Date date = new java.util.Date();
      %>
      Hello!  The time is now
      <%
        out.println( date );
        out.println( "<BR>Your machine's address is " );
        out.println( request.getRemoteHost());
      %>
  </BODY>
</HTML>
```

**Program4.jsp**

**Example program to print the table using for statement**

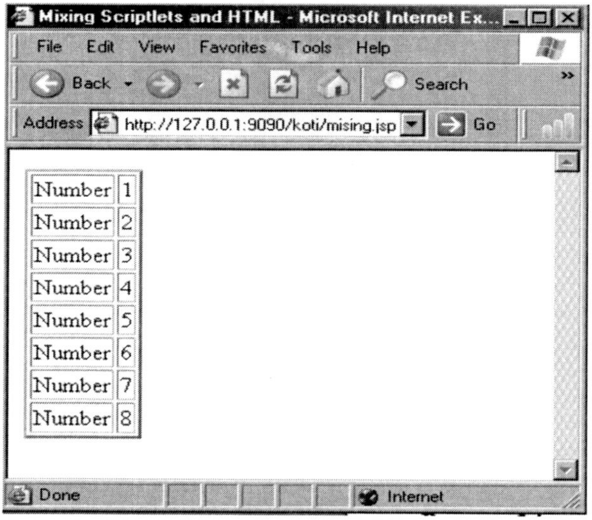


```
<html>
    <head>
        <title> Mixing Scriptlets and HTML</title>
```

```
    </head>
    <body>
        <TABLE BORDER=10>
        <%    for ( int i = 0; i < 8; i++ ) {       %>
            <TR>
            <TD>Number</TD>
            <TD><%= i+1 %></TD>
            </TR>
            <% }
        %>
        </TABLE>
    </body>
</html>
```

**hello.jsp**

**Display the current date and time.**

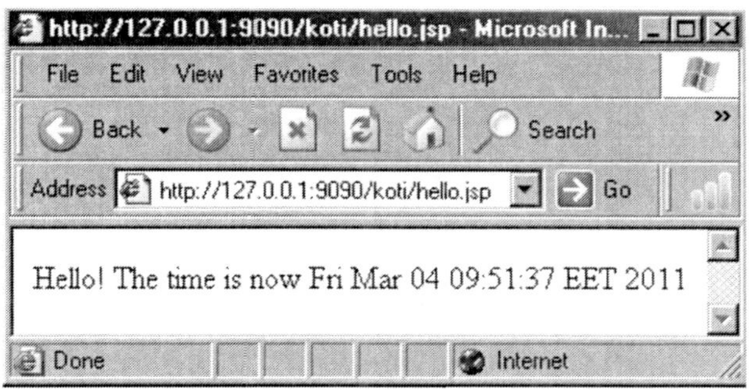


```
<%@ page import="java.util.*" %>
<HTML>
    <BODY>
        <%
          out.println( "Evaluating date now" );
           Date date = new Date();
        %>
        Hello!  The time is now <%= date %>
    </BODY>
</HTML>
```

**Hello1.jsp**

**Example program for using include element**

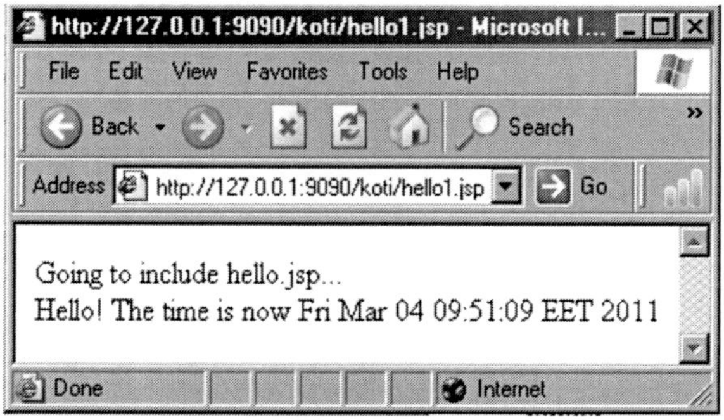


```
<HTML>
    <BODY>
        Going to include hello.jsp...<BR>
        <%@ include file="hello.jsp" %>
    </BODY>
</HTML>
```

**ValidationAlertMessage.jsp**

```
<html>
    <head>
      <script>
      function validLogin(){
      if (document.form.userName.value == ""){
      alert ( "Please enter Login Name." );
      document.loginform.userName.focus();
      return false;
      }
      if (document.form.password.value == ""){
      alert ( "Please enter password." );
      document.userform.password.focus();
      return false;
      }
      alert ( "Welcome User" );
      return true;
      }
      </script>
    </head>
    <body>
      <form name="form" method="post" onsubmit="return validLogin();">
      <center>User Login</center>
      Login Name: <input type="text" name="userName" value=""><br><br>
      Password: <input type="password" name="password" value="">
      <input type="submit" name="Submit" value="Login">
      </form>
    </body>
    </html>
```

**Previous question**: Write a JSP that allows the user to select an item from a list and to press submit button later prints the item on web page.

**jspCheckBox.jsp**

```
<html>
  <body>
      <h2>Select Languages:</h2>
```

```
        <form ACTION="jspCheckBox.jsp">
        <input type="checkbox" name="id" value="Java"> Java<BR>
        <input type="checkbox" name="id" value=".NET"> .NET<BR>
        <input type="checkbox" name="id" value="PHP"> PHP<BR>
        <input type="checkbox" name="id" value="C/C++"> C/C++<BR>
        <input type="checkbox" name="id" value="PERL"> PERL <BR>
        <input type="submit" value="Submit">
        </form>
        <%
        String select[] = request.getParameterValues("id");
        if (select != null && select.length != 0)
        {
           out.println("You have selected: ");
             for (int i = 0; i < select.length; i++)
             {
                out.println(select[i]);
             }
        }
        %>
    </body>
</html>
```

**JSP Application Design with MVC (**Model-View- Controller).

- The MVC architecture is one way to approach web application design.
- This uses a controller page to handle all requests
- The controller reads any query or form parameters
- Decides on which action to take, then dispatches control to another page to take the action.

## 4.8. MVC Architecture

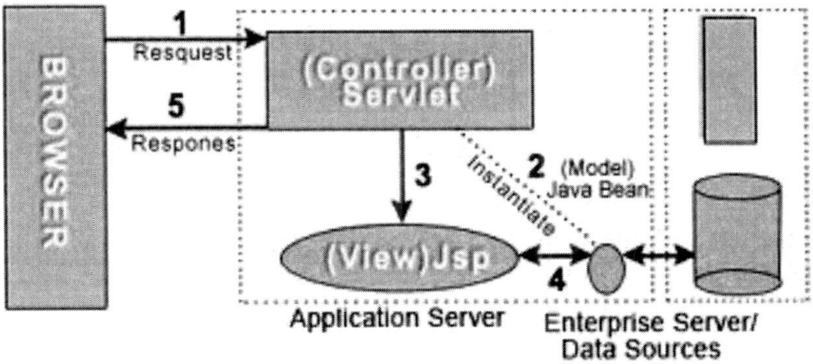


- The key point of using MVC is to separate components into three distinct units: the Model, the View, and the Controller.
- In a server application, we commonly classify the parts of the application as: business logic, presentation, and request processing.
- ***Business logic*** is the term used for the manipulation of an application's data, i.e., customer, product, and order information.
- ***Presentation*** refers to how the application is displayed to the user, i.e., the position, font, and size.
- ***Request processing*** is what ties the business logic and presentation parts together.
- In MVC terms, the **Model corresponds to business logic** and data, the **View to the presentation logic**, and the **Controller to the request processing**.
- MVC model is used for most of the examples. Many types of real-world applications can be developed this way.
- JSP pages are used as both the Controller and the View, and JavaBeans components are used as the Model.

**Example: JSP Page Showing the Current Date and Time (date.jsp)**

```
<%@ page language="java" contentType="text/html" %>
<html>
    <body bgcolor="white">
        <jsp:useBean id="clock" class="java.util.Date" />
        The current time at the server is:
        <ul>
            <li>Date: <jsp:getProperty name="clock" property="date" />
            <li>Month: <jsp:getProperty name="clock" property="month" />
            <li>Year: <jsp:getProperty name="clock" property="year" />
            <li>Hours: <jsp:getProperty name="clock" property="hours" />
            <li>Minutes: <jsp:getProperty name="clock" property="minutes" />
        </ul>
    </body>
</html>
```

The page shown in Example contains both regular HTML elements and JSP elements. The HTML elements are used as-is, defining the layout of the page.

- The first line in Example is a JSP *directive* element.

**<%@ page language="java" contentType="text/html" %>**

A JSP directive element starts with a directive-start identifier (**<%@** ) followed by the directive name (e.g., page) and directive attributes, and ends with **%>**. the language attribute value must be java, not Java.

- The contentType attribute specifies the type of content the page produces. The most common values are **text/html for HTML** content.
- Before you use a bean in a page, you must tell the JSP container which type of bean it is and associate it with a name. The first JSP action in Example, **<jsp:useBean>**, is used for this purpose:

**<jsp:useBean id="clock" class="java.util.Date" />**

➢ To include the current date property value in the page, use the following tag:

**<jsp:getProperty name="clock" property="date" />**

### *Installing the Java Software Development Kit*

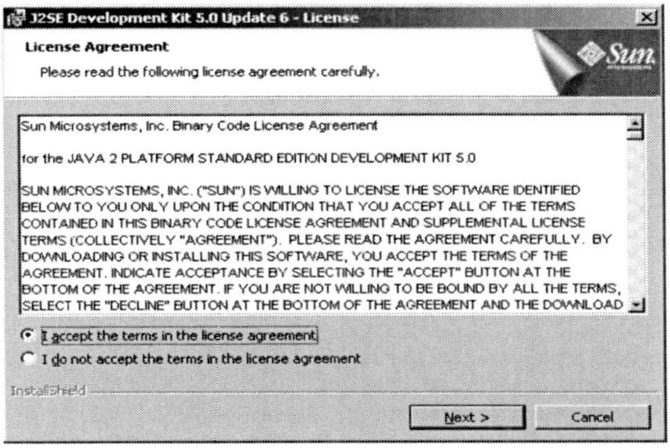


Tomcat is a pure Java web server with support for the Servlet and JSP specifications. To use it, you must first install a Java runtime environment. We can download a Java SDK for Windows, Linux, and Solaris at http://java.sun.com/j2se/. Once you have downloaded the j2se on your system, you are ready to install. In the following section we will learn how to install jdk development environment on your machine. Here are the step to install JDK on your windows machine.

### *Step 1*

Double click the JDK down loaded file, the executable extracts the required Contents to the temporary directory and then License agreement screen appears. On the license agreement page read and accept the license and the click the next button.

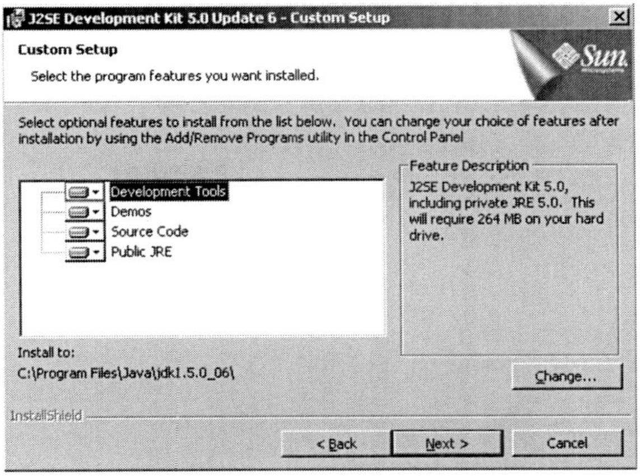

*Step 2*

The custom setup screen appears as follows.

*Step 3*

Click on the change button to change the installation directory to "**c:\jdk1.5.0_06**" as shown in the following screen, and click on the "OK" button. After clicking on the "OK" button installation begins.

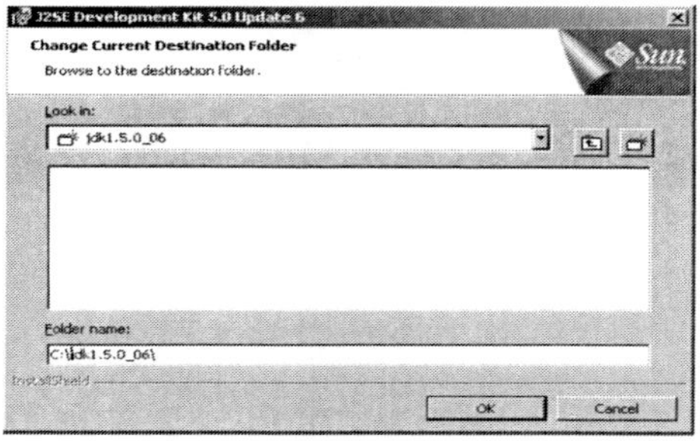


*Step 4*

In the next window installer asks for the installing the runtime as shown in the following screen:

*Step 5*

Click on next button install the J2SE runtime on your machine. Next

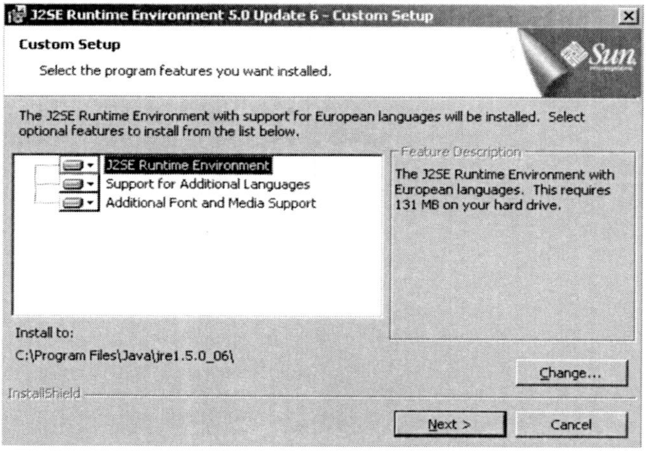

### *Step 6*

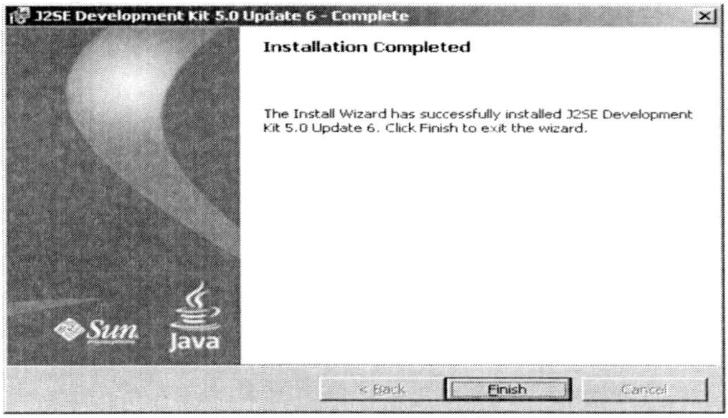


Once the installation is finished it shows you the final screen indications the success. Now you have successfully installed J2SE on your machine. Installer shows the following final confirmation window as shown below: Click on the "Finish" button to exit from the installer.

### *Configuring the Installation on Windows Machine*

In this Section we will add some settings to the windows environment so that the java compiler and runtime becomes available for compiling and running the java application. Go to the control panel and double click on "System Properties" and to to the advance tab. and add "c:\jdk1.5.0_06" to path variable:

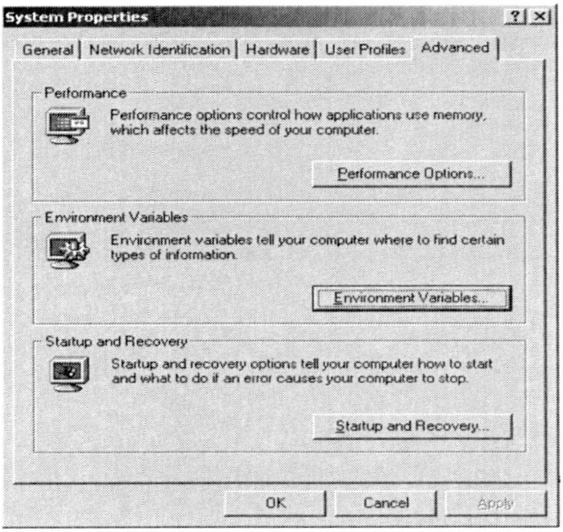

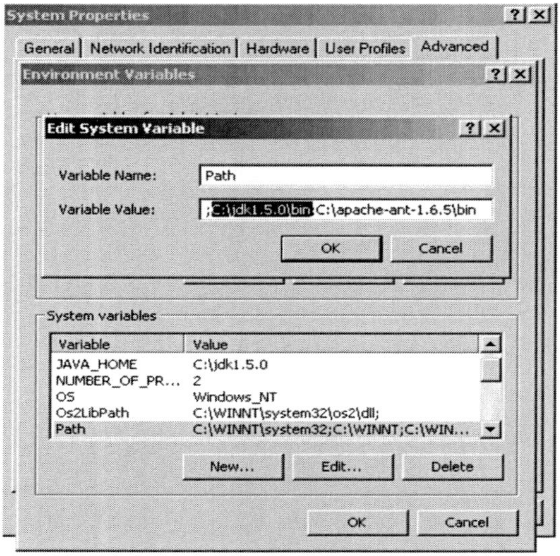


and click on ok button. To save the setting click on "OK" button. This will make the java environment available for development. Open the DOS prompt and type **java –version** on the console, it should show the following output:

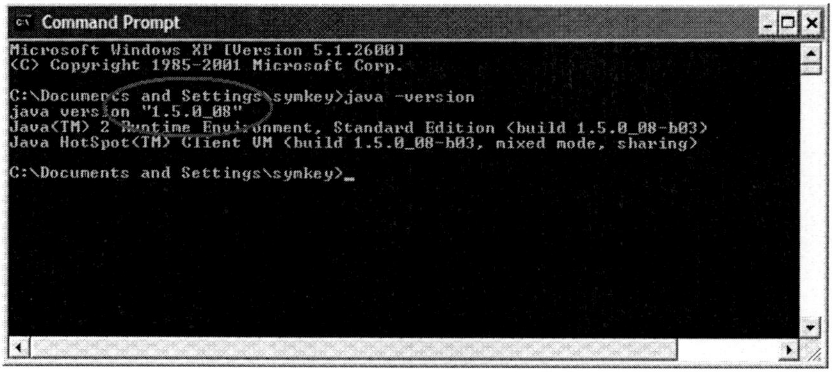


This indicates you have installed the JDK successfully.Now your development environment is ready for development.

### *Installing the Tomcat Server*

You can download the Tomcat Server either in binary format or as source code that you compile yourself, you should download the latest release.

The process of installing Tomcat 6.0 begins here from now. It takes various steps for installing and configuring the Tomcat 6.0.

For Windows OS, Tomcat comes in two forms: .zip file and .exe file (the Windows installer file). Here we are exploring the installation process by using the .exe file. First unpack the zipped file and simply execute the '.exe' file.

***Step 1***

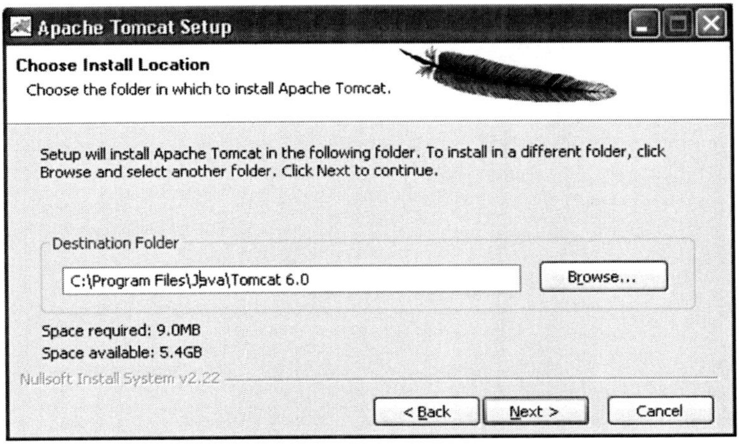


A Welcome screen shot appears that shows the beginning of installation process. Just click on the 'Next' button to proceed the installation process.

*Steps 2*

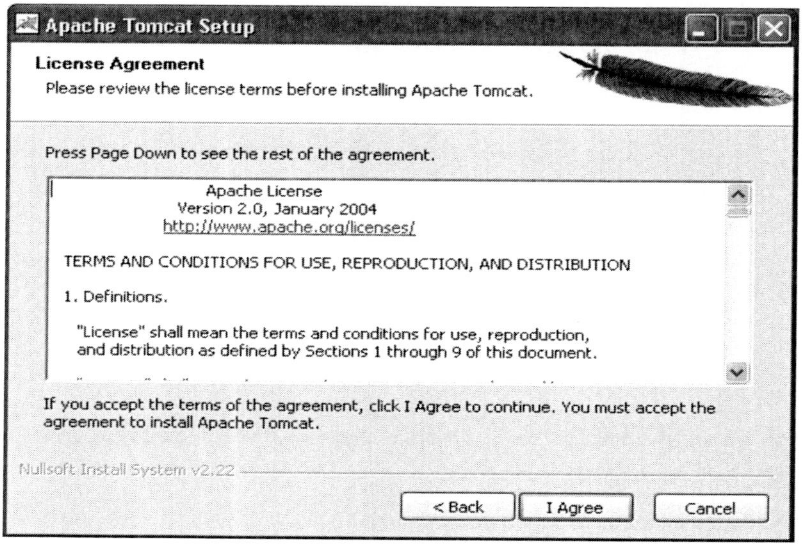


A screen of 'License Agreement' displays.

Click on the 'I Agree' button.

*Step 3*

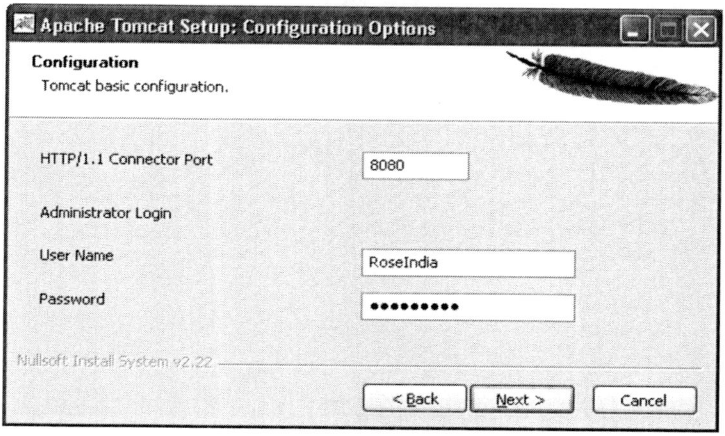


A screen shot appears asking for the 'installing location' Choose the default components and click on the 'Next' button.

*Step 4*

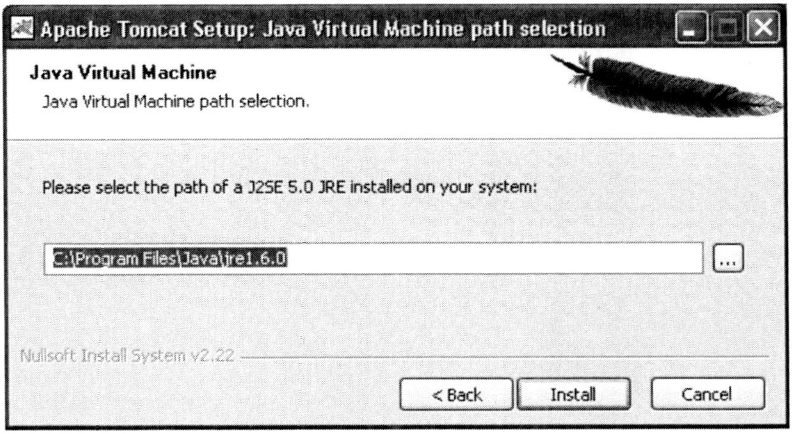


A screen shot of 'Configuration Options' displays on the screen. Choose the location for the Tomcat files as per your convenience. You can also opt the default Location. The port number will be your choice on which you want to run the tomcat server. The port number 8080 is the default port value for tomcat server to proceed the HTTP requests.

Now, click on the 'Next' button to further proceed the installation process.

*Step 7*

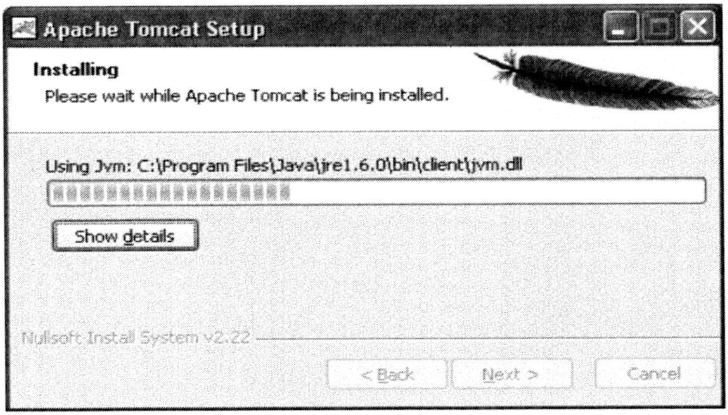


A Window of Java Virtual Machine displays on the screen. This window asks for the location of the installed Java Virtual Machine. Browse the location of the JRE folder and click on the Install button. This will install the Apache tomcat at the specified location.

***Step 8***

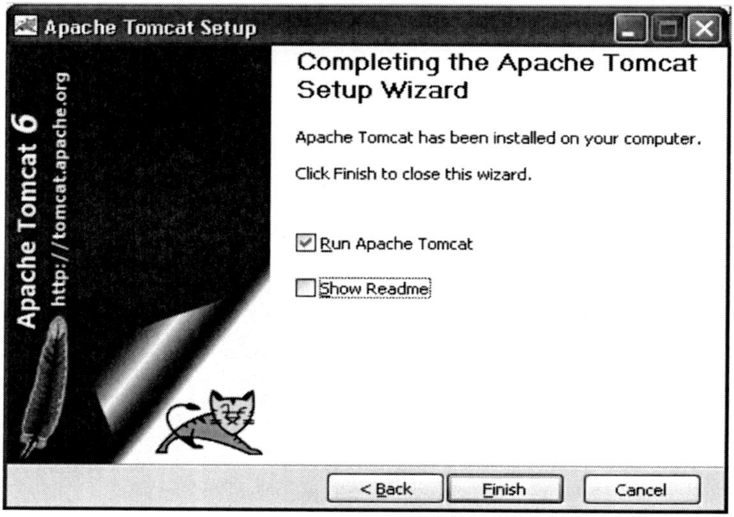


A processing window of installing displays on the screen. To get the information about installer click on the "Show details" button

***Step 9***

A screen shot of 'Tomcat Completion' displays on the screen. Click on the 'Finish' button.

***Step 10***

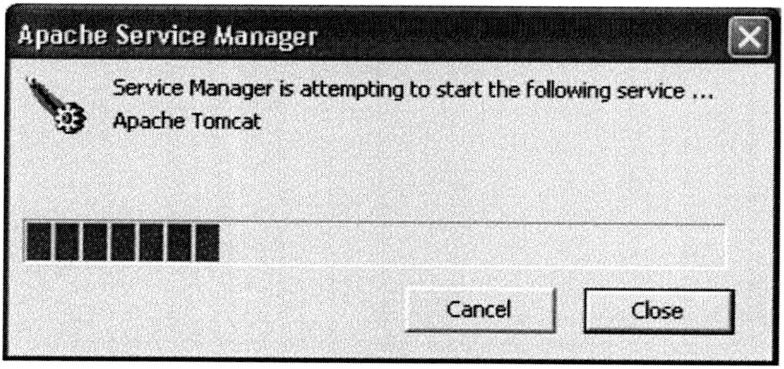


A window of Apache Service Manager appears with displaying the running process.

Let the running process goes on.

### *Step 11*

After completing the installation process, the Apache Tomcat Manager appears on the toolbar panel like shown in the below picture.

### *Testing Tomcat*

1. Start the tomcat server from the bin folder of Tomcat 6.0 directory by double clicking the "tomcat6.exe" file.

   OR

   Create a shortcut of this .exe file at your desktop.
2. Now Open web browser and type URL http://localhost:8080 in the address bar to test the server.
3. To Stop the Tomcat Server: Stop the server by pressing the "Ctrl + c" keys.

The screen of Apache Tomcat software looks like this:

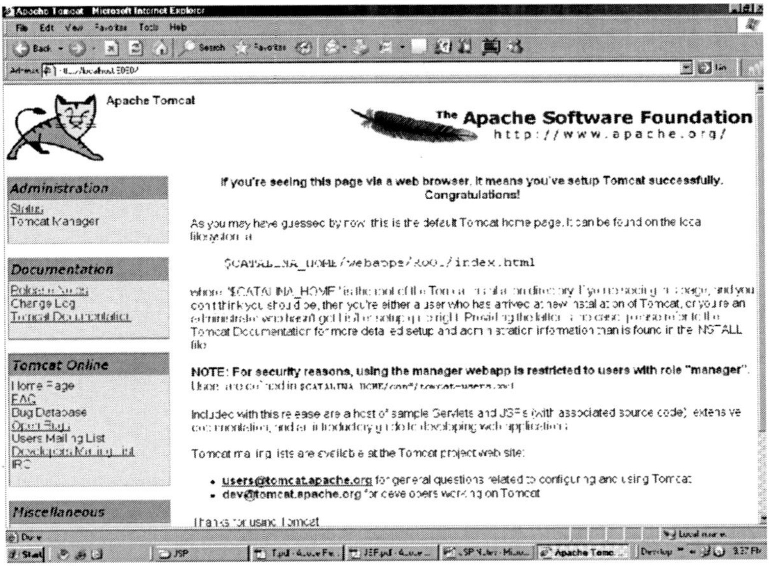

# UNIT V

# JSP APPLICATION DEVELOPMENT

## 5.1. Generating Dynamic Content

JSP page is just a regular HTML page with a few special elements. JSP pages should have the file extension ***.jsp***, which tells the server that the page needs to be processed by the JSP container. Without this clue, the server is unable to distinguish a JSP page from any other type of file and sends it unprocessed to the browser.

When working with JSP pages, you really just need a regular text editor such as Notepad on Windows or Emacs on UNIX. However, lists a number of tools that may make it easier for you, such as syntax aware editors that color-code JSP and HTML elements. Some Interactive Development Environments (IDEs) include a small web container that allows you to easily execute and debug the page during development.

JSP is all about **generating dynamic content**: content that differs based on user input, time of day, the state of an external system, or any other runtime conditions. JSP provides you with lots of tools for generating this content. We will learn about all of them - standard actions, custom actions, JavaBeans, and scripting elements. Before we do that, however, let's start with a few simple examples to get a feel for how the basic JSP elements work.

In this, we develop a page for displaying the current date and time, and look at the JSP directive element. Next, we look at how to process user input in your JSP pages and make sure it has the appropriate format.

The first example JSP page, named ***date.jsp***, is shown in Example.

**Example: JSP Page Showing the Current Date and Time (date.jsp)**

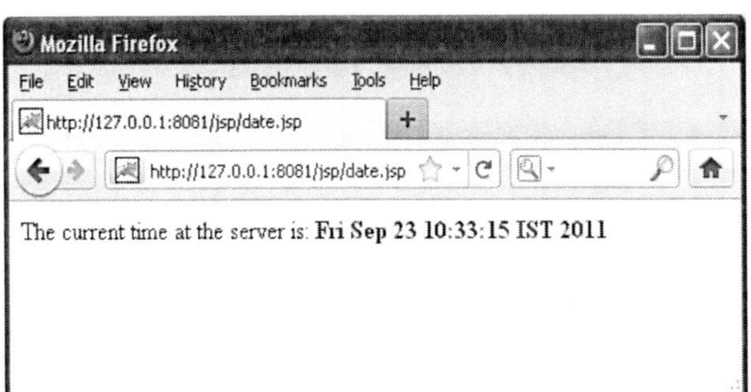

```
<%@ page import="java.util.Date" language="java" contentType="text/html" %>
<html>
<body bgcolor="white">
The current time at the server is:
<% Date date=new Date();
   out.println("<b>"+date);
%>
</body>
</html>
```

The ***date.jsp*** page displays the current date and time. We'll look at all the different pieces soon, but first let's run the example to see how it works. First start the Tomcat server and load the *http://localhost:8080/ora/date.jsp* URL in a browser. You should see a result like the one shown in Figure.

Notice that the month seems to be off by one and the year is displayed as 111. That's because the **java.util.Date** class we use here numbers months from 0 to 11, so January is 0, February is 1, and so on, and it reports year as the current year minus 1900. That's just the way this example works.

The page shown in Example contains both regular HTML elements and JSP elements. The HTML elements are used as-is, defining the layout of the page. If you use the View Source function in your browser, you notice that none of the JSP elements are visible in the page source.

## 5.2. Using JSP Directives

The first line in Example is a JSP *directive* element. Directives are used to specify attributes of the page itself, primarily those that affect how the page is converted into a Java servlet.

There are three JSP directives:

- page
- include
- taglib

In this example, we're using only the page directive. We'll see the others later. JSP pages typically start with a page directive that specifies the scripting language and the content type for the page:

```
<%@ page language="java" contentType="text/html" %>
```

A JSP directive element starts with a directive-start identifier (< %@) followed by the directive name (e.g., page) and directive attributes, and ends with %>. A directive contains one or more attribute name/value pairs (e.g., language="java"). Note that JSP element and attribute names are case-sensitive. For instance, the language attribute value must be "java", not "Java". All attribute values must also be enclosed in single or double quotes. The page directive has many possible attributes. In Example, two of them are used: language and contentType.

The language attribute specifies the scripting language used in the page. The JSP reference implementation (the Tomcat server) supports only Java as a scripting language. Java is also the default value for the language attribute, but for clarity you may still want to specify it.

The contentType attribute specifies the type of content the page produces. The most common values are text/html for HTML content and text/plain for preformatted, plain text. But you can also specify other types, such as text/xml for browsers that support XML.

## 5.3. JavaBeans Components in JSP Pages

Java Beans are reusable components. They are used to separate Business logic from the Presentation logic. Internally, a bean is just a java class.

JSP provides three basic tags for working with Beans.

- **<jsp:useBean id="*bean name*" class="bean class" scope = "page | request | session |application" />**

  bean name = the name that refers to the bean.

  Bean class = name of the java class that defines the bean.

- **<jsp:setProperty name = "id" property = "someProperty" value = "someValue" />**

  id = the name of the bean as specified in the useBean tag.

  property = name of the property to be passed to the bean.

  value = value of that particular property .

A variant for this tag is the property attribute can be replaced by an "*". What this does is that it accepts all the form parameters and thus reduces the need for writing multiple setProperty tags. The only consideration is that the form parameter names should be the same as that of the bean property names.

There are two ways to set JavaBeans component properties in a JSP page: with the jsp:setProperty element or with a scriptlet

**<% *beanName*.set*PropName*(*value*); %>**

The syntax of the jsp:setProperty element depends on the source of the property value. Table summarizes the various ways to set a property of a JavaBeans component using the jsp:setProperty element.

| **Setting JavaBeans Component Properties** | |
|---|---|
| **Value Source** | **Element Syntax** |
| String constant | <jsp:setProperty name="*beanName*" property="*propName*" value="*string constant*"/> |
| Request parameter | <jsp:setProperty name="*beanName*" property="*propName*" param="*paramName*"/> |
| Request parameter name matches bean property | <jsp:setProperty name="*beanName*" property="*propName*"/><br><jsp:setProperty name="*beanName*" property="*"/> |
| Expression | <jsp:setProperty name="*beanName*" property="*propName*" value="<%= *expression* %>"/> |
| 1. *beanName* must be the same as that specified for the id attribute in a useBean element.<br>2. There must be a *setPropName* method in the JavaBeans component.<br>3. *paramName* must be a request parameter name. | |

A property set from a constant string or request parameter must have a type listed in Table. Since both a constant and request parameter are strings, the Web container automatically converts the value to the property's type; the conversion applied is shown in the table. String values can be used to assign values to a property that has a PropertyEditor class. When that is the case, the setAsText(String) method is used. A conversion failure arises if the method throws an IllegalArgumentException.

| **Valid Value Assignments** | |
|---|---|
| **Property Type** | **Conversion on String Value** |
| Bean property | Uses setAsText(*string-literal*) |
| boolean or Boolean | As indicated in java.lang.Boolean.valueOf(String) |
| byte or Byte | As indicated in java.lang.Byte.valueOf(String) |
| char or Character | As indicated in java.lang.String.charAt(0) |
| double or Double | As indicated in java.lang.Double.valueOf(String) |
| int or Integer | As indicated in java.lang.Integer.valueOf(String) |
| float or Float | As indicated in java.lang.Float.valueOf(String) |
| long or Long | As indicated in java.lang.Long.valueOf(String) |
| short or Short | As indicated in java.lang.Short.valueOf(String) |
| Object | new String(*string-literal*) |

- **<jsp:getProperty name = "id" property = "someProperty" />**

Here the property is the name of the property whose value is to be obtained from the bean.

### *Object Scope*

Every JavaBean class object or any other class object we create will have a scope. Scope means the length of time this object will remain in memory.

There are four kinds of scopes:

- **Page** - it means a new object will be created and destroyed for every page view. This is the default for <jsp:useBean> tag when you don't explicitly give it any.
- **Request** - it means the newly created object will be created and bound to the request object. It is used in different JSP architectures.
- **Session** - the newly created object will be bound to the session object. What this means is that every visitor coming to your site will have a separate session for it, so you will not have to create a new object every time for it. You can just retrieve that object later again from the session object when you want it.
- **Application** - an object bound to application object means that your object will stay as long as the application remains loaded. This can be useful when for instance you want to count page views or daily sessions for your site.

## 5.4. The BEAN Structure

The most basic kind of bean simply exposes a number of properties by following a few simple rules regarding method names. The Java BEAN is not much different from a java program. The main differences are the signature methods being used in a bean. For passing parameters to a bean, there has to be a corresponding get/set method for every parameter. Together these methods are known as *assessors.*

### *Rules for Beans*

- Package should be first line of java bean.
- Bean should have an empty constructor.
- All the variables in a bean should have "get", "set" methods.
- The property name should start with an uppercase letter when used with "set", "get" methods. For example the variable "name" the get, set methods will be getName(), setName(String).
- Set method should return a void value like "return void()".

Example program for accessing the bean in jsp page is given bellow.

*MyBean.java*

```
package my;
public class MyBean
{
   private String name=new String();
   public MyBean(){}
   public String getName()
  {
       return name;
  }
  public void setName(String name)
  {
     this.name = name;
  }
}
```

*MyBean.jsp*

```
<html>
  <head>
     <title>Java bean example in jsp</title>
     <h1>Java bean example in jsp</h1>
     <hr></hr>
  </head>
  <body>
```

```
    <jsp:useBean id="mybean" class="my.MyBean" scope="session" >
    <jsp:setProperty name="mybean" property="name" value=" Hello world" />
    </jsp:useBean>
    <h1> <jsp:getProperty name="mybean" property="name" /></h1>
  </body>
</html>
```

In the above examples the bean that is being included is **MyBean.java** that has defined the set/get properties for the **"name"** object. Using the **MyBean.jsp** page first the bean is included using the **<jsp:useBean>** action, using the **<jsp:setProperty>** we set the property of **"name"** to **"Hello World"**. With the **<jsp:getProperty>** we get the value.

### *Using Scripting Elements*

We can create dynamic content by accessing java programming language objects from within scripting elements.

You can access a variety of objects, including enterprise beans and JavaBean components, within a JSP page. JSP technology automatically makes some objects available, and you can also create and access application-specific objects.

### *Implicit JSP Objects*

Implicit objects are created by the web container and contain information related to a particular request, page, or application. Many of the objects are defined by the Java Servlet technology underlying JSP technology.

Implicit object are those objects which are available in jsp by default. Developer does not need to declare these objects, the web container creates them. The following table is the list of jsp implicit objects.

Implicit JSP Object

| Variable Name | Java Type |
|---|---|
| request | javax.servlet.http.HttpServletRequest |
| response | javax.servlet.http.HttpServletResponse |
| pageContext | javax.servlet.jsp.PageContext |
| session | javax.servlet.http.HttpSession |
| application | javax.servlet.ServletContext |
| out | javax.servlet.jsp.JspWriter |
| config | javax.servlet.ServletConfig |
| page | java.lang.Object |
| exception | java.lang.Throwable |

Here is some more information about each of these implicit objects:

**Request:** The request object is an instance of the class named javax.servlet.http.HttpServlet Request. This object provides methods that let you access all the information that's available about the current request, such as request parameters, attributes, headers, and cookies.

**Response:** The response object represents the current response message. It's an instance of the javax.servlet.http.HttpServletResponse class, with methods for setting headers and the status code and for adding cookies. It also provides methods related to session tracking. These methods are the response methods you're most likely to use.

**Session:** The session object allows you to access the client's session data, managed by the server. It's an instance of the javax.servlet.http.HttpSession class. Typically you do not need to directly access this object, since JSP also lets you access the session data through action elements.

**Application:** The application object is another object that you typically access indirectly through action elements. It's an instance of the javax.servlet.ServletContext class. This object is used to hold references to other objects that more than one user may require access to, such as a database connection shared by all application users.

**Out:** The out object is an instance of javax.servlet.jsp.JspWriter. You can use the print( ) and println( ) methods provided by this object to add text to the response message body. We look at an example of this later in this chapter. In most cases, however, you will just use template text and JSP action elements instead of explicitly printing to the out object.

**Exception:** The exception object is available only in error pages and contains information about a runtime error.

The remaining three implicit objects (pageContext, config, and page) are so rarely used in scripting elements that we will not discuss them here.

### *Application-Specific Objects*

When possible, application behavior should be encapsulated in objects so that page designers can focus on presentation issues. Objects can be created by developers who are proficient in the Java programming language and in accessing databases and other services. There are four ways to create and use objects within a JSP page:

- Instance and class variables of the JSP page's servlet class are created in *declarations* and accessed in *scriptlets* and *expressions.*

- Local variables of the JSP page's servlet class are created and used in *scriptlets* and *expressions.*
- Attributes of scope objects (see Using Scope Objects) are created and used in *scriptlets* and *expressions.*
- JavaBeans components can be created and accessed using streamlined JSP elements. You can also create a JavaBeans component in a declaration or scriptlet and invoke the methods of a JavaBeans component in a scriptlet or expression.

Declarations, scriptlets, and expressions are described in JSP Scripting Elements.

### Shared Objects

The conditions affecting concurrent access to shared objects described in Sharing Information apply to objects accessed from JSP pages that run as multithreaded servlets. You can indicate how a Web container should dispatch multiple client requests with the following page directive:

```
<%@ page isThreadSafe="true|false" %>
```

When is ThreadSafe is set to true, the Web container may choose to dispatch multiple concurrent client requests to the JSP page. This is the *default* setting. If using true, you must ensure that you properly synchronize access to any shared objects defined at the page level. This includes objects created within declarations, JavaBeans components with page scope, and attributes of the page scope object.

If isThreadSafe is set to false, requests are dispatched one at a time, in the order they were received, and access to page-level objects does not have to be controlled. However, you still must ensure that access to attributes of the application or session scope objects and to JavaBeans components with application or session scope is properly synchronized.

### JSP Scripting Elements

JSP scripting elements are used to create and access objects, define methods, and manage the flow of control. Since one of the goals of JSP technology is to separate static template data from the code needed to dynamically generate content, very sparing use of JSP scripting is recommended. Much of the work that requires the use of scripts can be eliminated by using custom tags, described in Extending the JSP Language.

JSP technology allows a container to support any scripting language that can call Java objects. If you wish to use a scripting language other than the default, java, you must specify it in a page directive at the beginning of a JSP page:

```
<%@ page language="scripting language" %>
```

Since scripting elements are converted to programming language statements in the JSP page's servlet class, you must import any classes and packages used by a JSP page. If the page language is java, you import a class or package with the page directive:

<%@ page import="*packagename.*, fully_qualified_classname*" %>

For example, the bookstore example page showcart.jsp imports the classes needed to implement the shopping cart with the following directive:

```
<%@ page import="java.util.*, cart.*" %>
```

### *Declarations*

A *JSP declaration* is used to declare variables and methods in a page's scripting language. The syntax for a declaration is as follows:

```
<%! scripting language declaration %>
```

When the scripting language is the Java programming language, variables and methods in JSP declarations become declarations in the JSP page's servlet class.

The given example defines an instance variable named **start** and the initialization and finalization methods **jspInit** and **jspDestroy** discussed earlier in a declaration:

```
<%!
  private int start;
  public void jspInit()
{
    ...
  }
  public void jspDestroy()
{
    ...
  }
%>
```

Scriptlets

A *JSP scriptlet* is used to contain any code fragment that is valid for the scripting language used in a page. The syntax for a scriptlet is as follows:

```
<%
  scripting language statements
%>
```

When the scripting language is set to java, a scriptlet is transformed into a Java programming language statement fragment and is inserted into the service method of the JSP page's servlet. A programming language variable created within a scriptlet is accessible from anywhere within the JSP page.

```
<%
  int a=10,b=20,c;
  c=a+b;
  out.println("The result is: "+c);
%>
```

### *Displaying Values Using an Expression*

A JSP expression is used to insert values directly into the output. It has the following form:

**<%= *Java Expression* %>**

The expression is evaluated, converted to a string, and inserted in the page. This evaluation is performed at run time (when the page is requested) and thus has full access to information about the request.

For example, the following shows the date/time that the page was requested:

Current time: **<%= new java.util.Date() %>**

### *Example*

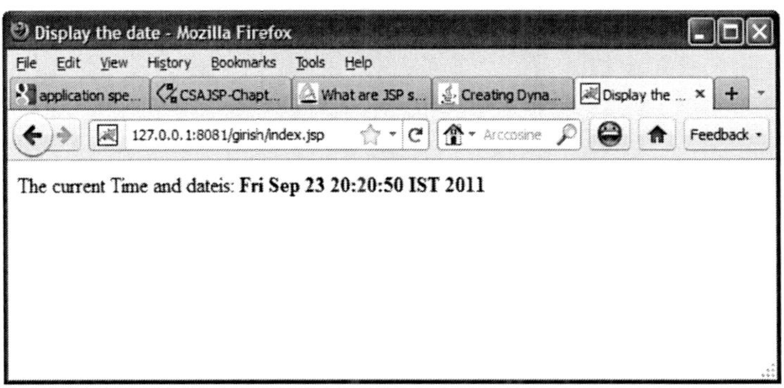


```
<%@ page language="java" contentType="text/html" %>
<html>
<head>
<title> Display the date </title>
```

```
</head>
<body>
<%=new java.util.Date()%>
</body>
</html>
```

In the above program we used the expression element **<%=new java.util.Date()%>.** Here that can display the time and date on the web browser.

### *Using an Expression to Set an Attribute*

In all our JSP action element examples so far, the attributes are set to literal string values. But in many cases, the value of an attribute is not known when you write the JSP page; instead, the value must be calculated when the JSP page is requested. For situations like this, you can use a JSP expression as an attribute value. This is called a *request-time attribute value.*

Here is an example of how this can be used to set an attribute of a fictitious log entry bean:

```
<jsp:useBean id="logEntry" class="java.util.Date" />
<jsp:setProperty name="logEntry" property="entryTime"
value="<%= new java.util.Date( ) %>" />
```

This bean has a property named **entryTime** that holds a timestamp for a log entry, while other properties hold the information to be logged. To set the timestamp to the time when the JSP page is requested, a **<jsp:setProperty>** action with a request-time attribute value is used. The attribute value is represented by the same type of JSP expression as in the previous snippet, here an expression that creates a new **java.util.Date** object (representing the current date and time). The request time attribute is evaluated when the page is requested, and the corresponding attribute is set to the result of the expression.

### *Declaring Variables and Methods*

We have used two of the three JSP scripting elements: scriptlets and expressions. There's one more, called a *declaration element,* which is used to declare Java variables and methods in a JSP page. My advice is don't use it. Let me explain why. Java variables can be declared either within a method or outside the body of all methods, like this:

```
public class SomeClass
{
// Instance variable
private String anInstanceVariable;
```

```
// Method
public void doSomething( )
{
String aLocalVariable;
}
}
```

A variable declared outside the body of all methods is called an *instance variable.* Its value can be accessed from any method in the class, and it keeps its value even when the method that sets it returns. A variable declared within the body of a method is called a *local variable.* A local variable can be accessed only from the method where it's declared. When the method returns, the local variable disappears.

When you declare a variable within a scriptlet element instead of in a JSP declaration block, the variable ends up as a local variable in the generated servlet's request processing method. Each thread has its own copy of a local variable, so local variables can't cause any problems if more than one thread executes the same code. If the value of a local variable is changed, it will not affect the other threads.

That being said, let's look at a simple example. We use two int variables: one declared as an instance variable using a JSP expression, and the other declared as a local variable. We increment them both by one and display the new values.

Example shows the test page.

### *Example. Using a Declaration Element (counter.jsp)*

```
<%@ page language="java" contentType="text/html" %>
<%!
int globalCounter = 0;
%>
<html>
<head>
<title>A page with a counter</title>
</head>
<body bgcolor="white">
This page has been visited: <%= ++globalCounter %> times.
<p>
<%
```

```
int localCounter = 0;
%>
This counter never increases its value: <%= ++localCounter %>
</body>
</html>
```

The JSP declaration element is right at the beginning of the page, starting with <%! and ending with %>. Note the exclamation point (!) in the start identifier; that's what makes it a declaration as opposed to a scriptlet. The declaration element declares an instance variable named globalCounter, shared by all requests for the page. In the body section of the page, JSP expression increments the variable's value. Next comes a scriptlet, enclosed by <% and %>, that declares a local variable named localCounter. The last scriptlet increments the value of the local variable.

## 5.5. Error Handling and Debugging

Exceptions mean exceptional events and as we all know exceptional events can occur anywhere in a program e.g. you are trying to connect to a database and the database server is down, now you wouldn't have expected which can be display.

### *How to Catch Exceptions?*

You can catch exceptions in a JSP page like you would do in other Java classes. Simply put the code which can throw an exception/s between a try..Catch block.

There is yet another useful way of catching exceptions in JSP pages. You can specify error page in the **'page'** directive. Then if any exception is thrown, the control will be transferred to that error page where you can display a useful message to the user about what happened and also inform your system admin about this exception depending obviously on how important it may be. In this article we will explore this error page method of exception handling in JSP pages.

### *Building Demo Pages*

To demonstrate the run-time exception handling feature of JSP pages, we will build three pages.

- Form.html - Display a Form to the user to enter his or her age.
- FormHandler.jsp - A JSP Page which receives this value and prints it on the user screen.
- ExceptionHandler.jsp - An exception handler JSP page which is actually an error page to which control will be passed when an exception is thrown.

### 1. *Form.html*

Create a new Form.html page. Copy the following code and paste it into the Form.html page:

```
<html>
<head>
    <style>
    body, input { font-family:Tahoma; font-size:8pt; }
    </style>
</head>
<body>
<!-- HTML Form -->
<form action="FormHandler.jsp" method="post">
    Enter your age ( in years ) :
    <input type="text" name="age" />
    <input type="submit" value="Submit" />
</form>
</body>
</html>
```

#### *Explanation*

Form.html page simply displays a single input field Form to the user to enter his age in years. The name of input field where user will enter age is "age". We will use this input field name "age" in the FormHandler.jsp page to receive its value.

### 2. *FormHandler.jsp*

Create new FormHandler.jsp page.

```
<%@ page errorPage="ExceptionHandler.jsp" %>
<html>
<head>
    <style>
    body, p { font-family:Tahoma; font-size:10pt; }
    </style>
</head>
<body>
<%-- Form Handler Code --%>
<%
```

```
    int age;
    age = Integer.parseInt(request.getParameter("age"));
%>
 <%-- Displaying User Age --%>
<p>Your age is : <%= age %> years.</p>
<p><a href="Form.html">Back</a>.</p>
 </body></html>
```

### *Explanation*

Code above is rather simple. Notice the first line, the page directive. It specifies an errorPage ExceptionHandler.jsp, our exception handler JSP page.

```
<%@ page errorPage="ExceptionHandler.jsp" %>
```

Then we declare an int variable "age". Then using the static method of Integer class we parse the entered value using Integer.parseInt() method. The value is retrieved using request.getParameter() method. The argument to request.getParameter() is the name of Form field whose value we want to retrieve.

```
<%
    int age;
    age = Integer.parseInt(request.getParameter("age"));
%>
```

If all goes well and user entered an int (e.g. 12345) value in the input field then we display that value back to the user.

```
<p>Your age is : <%= age %> years.</p>
```

Now things can go wrong and exceptional events can occur. For example, if user didn't enter a value and what if user entered his name (e.g. "Faisal Khan"), of String type instead of an integer.

These things will be handled by the ExceptionHandler.jsp JSP page.

### *3. ExceptionHandler.jsp*

Create a new ExceptionHandler.jsp page.

```
<%@ page isErrorPage="true" import="java.io.*" %>
<html>
<head>
    <title>Exceptional Even Occurred!</title>
```

```
</head>
<body>
 <%-- Exception Handler --%>
<font color="red">
<%= exception.toString() %><br>
</font>
 <%
out.print("Enter Numbers only not a string"); %>
 </body>
</html>
```

### *Explanation*

To make a JSP page exception handler ( i.e. errorPage ), you have to specify isErrorPage attribute in the page directive at the top and set its value to true.

```
<%@ page isErrorPage="true" %>
```

When a JSP page has been declared an errorPage, it is made available an object with name of "exception" of type java.lang.Throwable. We use different methods of this exception object to display useful information to the user.

```
<font color="red">
    <%= exception.toString() %><br>
</font>
```

We can put the stack trace information for debugging inside HTML <!-- --> comment tags. So that user only sees a useful message and the sysadmin, developers can see the whole story.

Enter your age e.g. 24, in the input field and press the submit button. You should see FormHandler.jsp page giving you a response like following:

Your age is : 24 years.

Now try again. This time don't enter any value or simply enter a non-integer value e.g. your name, and press the submit button. Now instead of FormHandler.jsp page showing you your age, the control will be internally passed to ExceptionHandler.jsp page which will show an exception message in red color:

java.lang.NumberFormatException:

To see the complete stack trace views the source of the page. On Internet Explorer, click View -> Source. On the source page you will see complete exception stack trace written.

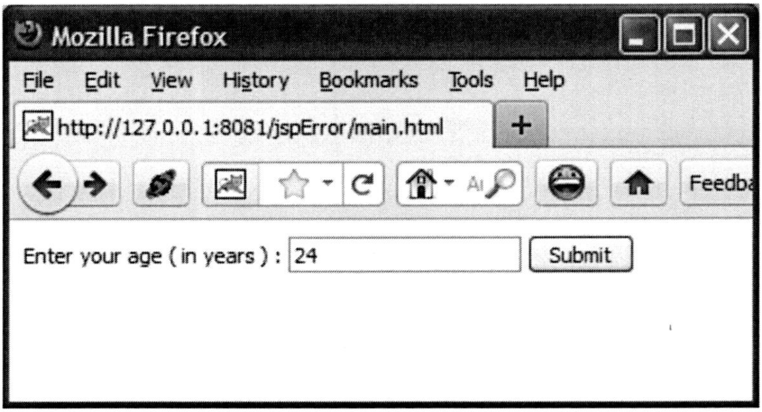
Mozilla Firefox
File Edit View History Bookmarks Tools Help
http://127.0.0.1:8081/jspError/main.html
Enter your age ( in years ) : 24
Submit

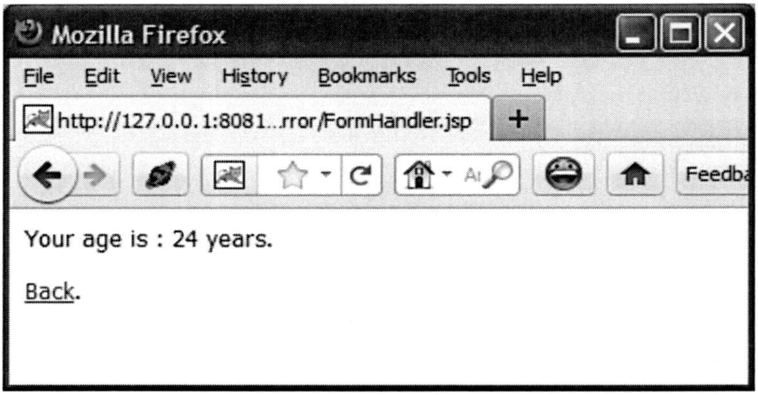
Mozilla Firefox
File Edit View History Bookmarks Tools Help
http://127.0.0.1:8081...rror/FormHandler.jsp
Your age is : 24 years.
Back.

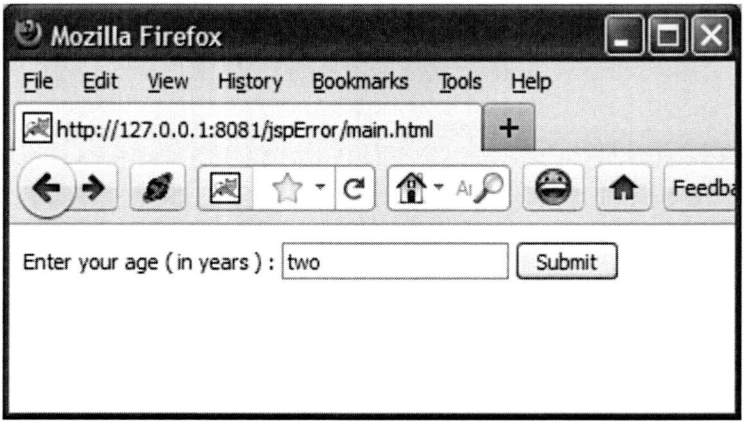
Mozilla Firefox
File Edit View History Bookmarks Tools Help
http://127.0.0.1:8081/jspError/main.html
Enter your age ( in years ) : two
Submit

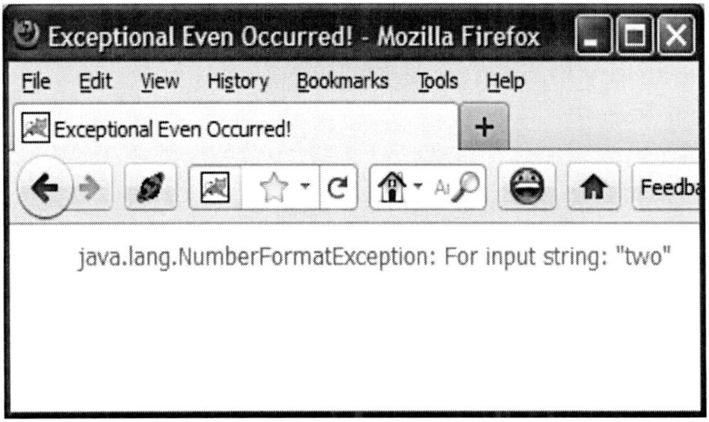


## 5.6. Sharing Data between JSP Pages

One of the most fundamental features of JSP technology is that it allows for separation of request processing, business logic, and presentation, using what's known as the Model-View-Controller (MVC) model. As you may recall, the roles of Model, View, and Controller can be assigned to different types of server-side components. JSP pages are used for both the Controller and View roles and the Model role is played by either a bean or a JSP page. This is not necessarily the best approach, but it lets us focus on JSP features instead of getting into Java programming. Using different JSP pages as Controller and View means that more than one page is used to process a request.

To make this happen, you need to be able to do two things:

1. Pass control from one page to another.
2. Pass data from one page to another.

In this section, we look at a concrete example of how to separate the different aspects of an application and how JSP supports the two requirements above. Let's revisit the User Info example, to describe how the different aspects of an application can be separated. In this example, the business logic piece is trivial.

We can categorize the different aspects of the User Info example like this:

Display the form for user input (presentation).

- Validate the input (request processing and business logic).
- Display the result of the validation (presentation).

Let's use a separate JSP page for each aspect. The restructured application contains three JSP pages, as shown in Figure.

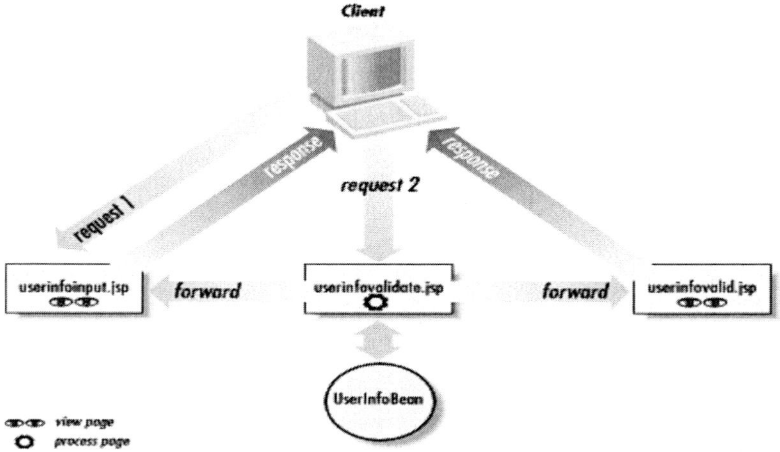


User Info Application Pages

Here's how it works. The *userinfoinput.jsp* page displays an input form. The user submits this form to *userinputvalidate.jsp* to validate the input. This page processes the request using the UserInfoBean and passes control (forwards) to either the *userinfoinput.jsp* page (if the input is invalid) or the *userinfovalid.jsp* page (if the input is valid). If valid, the *userinfovalid.jsp* page displays a "thank you" message. In this example, the UserInfoBean represents the Model, the *userinputvalidate.jsp* page the Controller, and *userinfoinput.jsp* and *userinfovalid.jsp* represent the Views.

This gives you the flexibility and maintainability. If the validation rules change, a Java programmer can change the UserInfoBean implementation without touching any other part of the application. If the customer wants a different look, a page author can modify the View JSP pages without touching the request processing or business logic code.

### *Transferring Control to Another Web Component*

The mechanism for transferring control to another Web component from a JSP page uses the functionality provided by the Java Servlet API as described in Transferring Control to Another Web Component. You access this functionality from a JSP page with the **jsp:forward** element:

**<jsp:forward page="** userinfovalid.jsp" **/>**

Note that if any data has already been returned to a client, the jsp:forward element will fail with an IllegalStateException.

### *Param Element*

When an include or forward element is invoked, the original request object is provided to the target page. If you wish to provide additional data to that page, you can append parameters to the request object with the jsp:param element:

```
<jsp:include page="..." >
  <jsp:param name="param1" value="value1"/>
</jsp:include>
```

## 5.7. Passing Data from One Page to Another

JSP provides different *scopes* for sharing data objects between pages, requests, and users. The scope defines for how long the object is available and whether it's available only to one user or to all application users.

The following scopes are defined:

Page

- Request
- Session
- Application

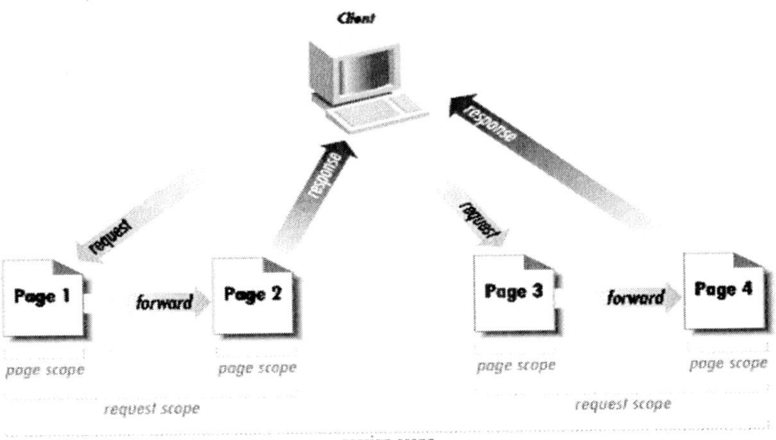


Lifetime of Objects in Different Scopes

Objects placed in the default scope, the *page scope*, are available only to actions and scriptlets within one page. That's the scope used in all examples you have seen so far. The *request scope* is for objects that need to be available to all pages processing the same request. The *session scope* is for objects shared by multiple requests by the same user, and the *application scope* is for objects shared by all users of the application.

## 5.8. Sharing Session and Application Data

HTTP is a stateless, request-response protocol. This means that the browser sends a request for a web resource, and the web server processes the request and returns a response. The server then forgets this transaction ever happened. So when the same browser sends a new request, the web server has no idea that this request is related to the previous one. This is fine if you're dealing with static files, but it's a problem in an interactive web application. In a travel agency application, for instance, it's important to remember the dates and destination entered to book the flight so the customer doesn't have to enter the same information again when it's time to make hotel and rental car reservations.

The way to solve this problem is to let the server send a piece of information to the browser that the browser then includes in all subsequent requests. This piece of information, called a session ID, is used by the server to recognize a set of requests from the same browser as related: in other words, as part of the same session. A session starts when the browser makes the first request for a JSP page in a particular application. The session can be ended explicitly by the application, or the JSP container can end it after a period of user inactivity (the default value is typically 30 minutes after the last request).

JSP hides most of the details about how the session ID is transferred and how the session object is created and accessed, providing you with the session scope to handle session data at a convenient level of abstraction. Information saved in the session scope is available to all pages requested by the same browser during the lifetime of the session.

However, some information is needed by multiple pages independent of who the current user is. JSP supports access to this type of shared information through another scope, the application scope. Information saved in the application scope by one page can later be accessed by another page, even if the two pages were requested by different users. Examples of information typically shared through the application scope are database connection pool objects, information about currently logged-in users, and cache objects to avoid frequent database lookups.

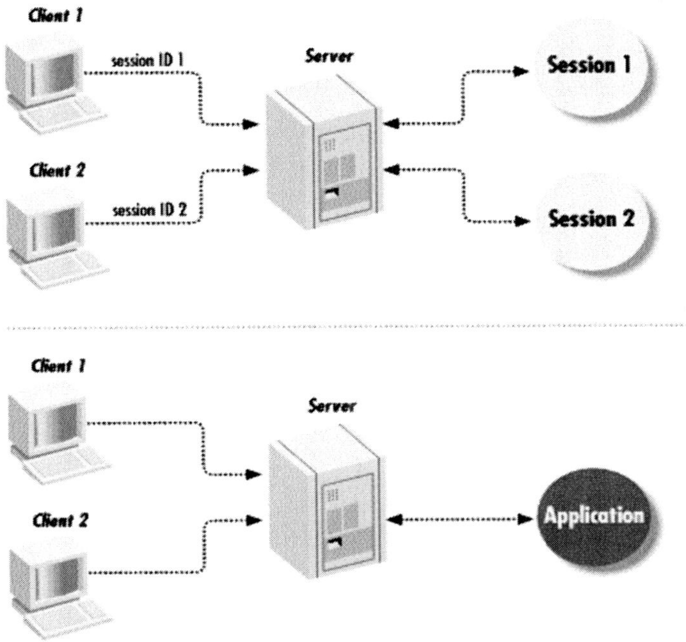


Session and Application Scopes

## 5.9. Counting Page Hits

A simple page counter bean can be used to illustrate how the scope affects the lifetime and reach of shared information. The difference between the two scopes becomes apparent when you place the bean in both the session and application scopes. Consider the page shown in Example.

### *Example. Page with Counter Beans (counter1.jsp)*

```
<%@ page language="java" contentType="text/html"%>
<html>
 <body>
        <jsp:useBean id="counter" scope="application" class="beans.Counter" />
  <center><b>The current count for the counter bean is: </b>
   <%=counter.getCount() %></center>
 </body>
</html>
```

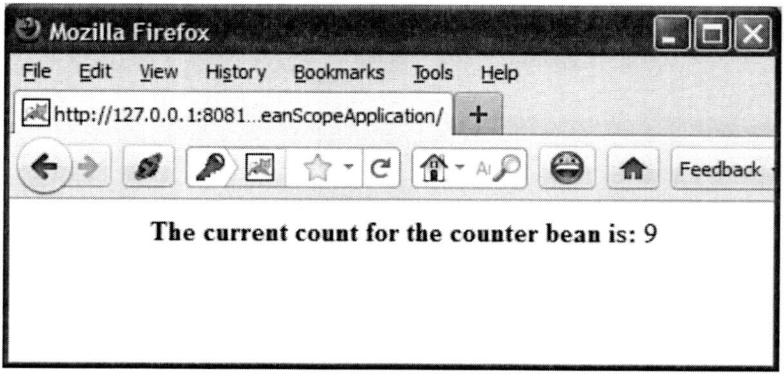


### *Including Content in a JSP Page*

There are two mechanisms for including another Web resource in a JSP page: the **include** directive and the **jsp:include** element.

The include directive is processed when the JSP page is *translated* into a servlet class. The effect of the directive is to insert the text contained in another file--either static content or another JSP page--in the including JSP page.

The syntax for the include directive is as follows:

```
<%@ include file="filename" %>
```

For example, all the bookstore application pages include the file banner.jsp containing the banner content with the following directive:

```
<%@ include file="banner.jsp" %>
```

Because you must statically put an include directive in each file that reuses the resource referenced by the directive, this approach has its limitations. For a more flexible approach to building pages out of content chunks, see A Template Tag Library.

The **jsp:include** element is processed when a JSP page is *executed.* The include action allows you to include either a static or dynamic resource in a JSP file. The results of including static and dynamic resources are quite different. If the resource is static, its content is inserted into the calling JSP file. If the resource is dynamic, the request is sent to the included resource, the included page is executed, and then the result is included in the response from the calling JSP page. The syntax for the **jsp:include** element is as follows:

```
<jsp:include page="includedPage" />
```

## 5.10. Memory Usage Considerations

You should be aware that all objects you save in the application and session scopes take up memory in the server process. It's easy to calculate how much memory is used for application objects since you have full control over the number of objects you place there. But the total number of objects in the session scope depends on the number of concurrent sessions, so in addition to the size of each object, you also need to know how many concurrent users you have and how long a session lasts. Let's look at an example. The CartBean used in this chapter is small. It stores only references to ProductBean instances, not copies of the beans. An object reference in Java is 8 bytes, so with three products in the cart we need 24 bytes. The java.util.Vector object used to hold the references adds some overhead, say 32 bytes. All in all, we need 56 bytes per shopping cart bean with three products.

If this site has a modest number of customers, you may have 10 users shopping per hour. The default timeout for a session is 30 minutes, so let's say that at any given moment, you have 10 active users and another 10 sessions that are not active but have not timed out yet. This gives a total of 20 sessions times 56 bytes per session, a total of 1,120 bytes. In other words, a bit more than 1 KB. That's nothing to worry about. Now let's say your site becomes extremely popular, with 2,000 customers per hour. Using the same method to calculate the number of concurrent sessions, you now have 4,000 sessions at 56 bytes, a total of roughly 220 KB - still nothing to worry about. However, if you store larger objects in each session, for instance the results of a database search, with an average of 10 KB per active session, that corresponds to roughly 40 MB for 4,000 sessions. A lot more, but still not extreme, at least not for a site intended to handle this amount of traffic. However, it should become apparent that with that many users, you have to be a bit more careful with how you use the session scope.

Here are some things you can do to keep the memory requirements under control:

- Place only those objects that really need to be unique for each session in the session scope. In the shopping cart example, for instance, each cart contains references only to the shared product beans, and the catalog bean is shared by all users.
- Set the timeout period for sessions to a lower value than the default. If you know it's rare that your users leave the site for 30 minutes and then return, use a shorter period. You can change the timeout for all sessions in an application through the application's Deployment Descriptor, or call session.setMax-Inactivelnterval( ) to change it for an individual session.

- Provide a way to end the session explicitly. A good example is a logout function. Another possibility is to invalidate the session when something is completed (such as submitting the order form). You can use the session.invalidate( ) method to invalidate a session and make all objects available for garbage collection (the term used when the Java runtime is allowed to remove unused objects to conserve memory).

# UNIT VI

# DATABASE ACCESS

## 6.1. JDBC

JDBC stands for **J**ava **Data**b**a**se **C**onnectivity, which is a standard Java API for database-independent connectivity between the Java programming language and a wide range of databases. The JDBC library includes APIs for each of the tasks commonly associated with database usage:

- Load the driver
- Making a connection to a database
- Creating SQL statements
- Executing that SQL queries in the database
- Viewing & Modifying the resulting records

You need to have good understanding on the following two subjects to learn JDBC:

1. Core JAVA Programming
2. SQL Database

JDBC - Environment Setup:

Make sure you have done following setup:

1. Core JAVA Installation
2. SQL Database Installation

Apart from the above you need to setup a database which you would use for your project. Assuming this is EMP and you have created on table Employees within the same database.

### *Creating JDBC Application*

There are six steps involved in building a JDBC application which are given briefly.

### *Import the Packages*

This requires that you include the packages containing the JDBC classes needed for database programming. Most often, using import java.sql.* will suffice as follows:

```
//STEP 1. Import required packages
import java.sql.*;
```

### *Register the JDBC Driver*

This requires that you initialize a driver so you can open a communications channel with the database. Following is the code snippet to achieve this:

```
//STEP 2: Register JDBC driver

Class.forName("sun.jdbc.odbc.JdbcOdbcDriver");
```

### *Open a Connection*

This requires using the DriverManager.getConnection() method to create a Connection object, which represents a physical connection with the database as follows:

### *Execute a Query*

This requires using an object of type Statement or PreparedStatement for building and submitting an SQL statement to the database as follows:

```
//STEP 4: Execute a query

Statement stmt = conn.createStatement();

String sql= "SELECT id, first, last, age FROM Employees";

ResultSet rs = stmt.executeQuery(sql);
```

If there is an SQL UPDATE, INSERT or DELETE statement required, then following code snippet would be required:

```
//STEP 4: Execute a query

System.out.println("Creating statement...");

Statement stmt = conn.createStatement();

String sql;

sql = "DELETE FROM Employees";

ResultSet rs = stmt.executeUpdate(sql);
```

### *Extract Data from Result Set*

This step is required in case you are fetching data from the database. You can use the appropriate ResultSet.getXXX() method to retrieve the data from the result set as follows:

```
    //STEP 5: Extract data from result set
while(rs.next()){
   //Retrieve by column name
   int id  = rs.getInt("id");
   int age = rs.getInt("age");
   String first = rs.getString("first");
   String last = rs.getString("last");
   //Display values
   System.out.print("ID: " + id);
   System.out.print(", Age: " + age);
   System.out.print(", First: " + first);
   System.out.println(", Last: " + last);
}
```

### *Clean up the Environment*

You should explicitly close all database resources versus relying on the JVM's garbage collection as follows:

```
//STEP 6: Clean-up environment
rs.close();
stmt.close();
conn.close();
```

### *First JDBC Program*

Based on the above steps, we can have following consolidated sample code which we can use as a template while writing our JDBC code:

This sample code has been written based on the environment and database setup done in Environment chapter.

```
//STEP 1. Import required packages
import java.sql.*;
public class FirstExample
{
     public static void main(String[] args) throws Exception
  {
   Connection conn = null;
```

```
Statement stmt = null;
try
{
  //STEP 2: Register JDBC driver
  Class.forName("oracle.jdbc.driver.OracleDriver");
  //STEP 3: Open a connection
  System.out.println("Connecting to database...");
 onn=DriverManager.getConnection("jdbc:oracle:thin:@localhost:1521:XE","system","tiger");
  //STEP 4: Execute a query
  System.out.println("Creating statement...");
  stmt = conn.createStatement();
  String sql = "SELECT id, first, last, age FROM Employees";
  ResultSet rs = stmt.executeQuery(sql);
  //STEP 5: Extract data from result set
  while(rs.next())
  {
    //Retrieve by column name
    int id  = rs.getInt("id");
    int age = rs.getInt("age");
    String first = rs.getString("first");
    String last = rs.getString("last");
    //Display values
    System.out.print("ID: " + id);
    System.out.print(", Age: " + age);
    System.out.print(", First: " + first);
    System.out.println(", Last: " + last);
  }
  //STEP 6: Clean-up environment
  rs.close();
  stmt.close();
  conn.close();
}
catch(SQLException se)
{
```

```
    //Handle errors for JDBC
    se.printStackTrace();
  }
 }//end try
  System.out.println("Goodbye!");
}//end main
}//end FirstExample
```

Now let us compile above example as follows:

```
C:\>javac FirstExample.java
C:\>
```

When you run **FirstExample**, it produces following result:

```
C:\>java FirstExample
Connecting to database...
Creating statement...
ID: 100, Age: 18, First: Zara, Last: Ali
ID: 101, Age: 25, First: Mahnaz, Last: Fatma
ID: 102, Age: 30, First: Zaid, Last: Khan
ID: 103, Age: 28, First: Sumit, Last: Mittal
C:\>
```

### *Steps to connect JDBC-ODBC bridge driver with database*

**Step1:-** First, create a database using "MS Access", which must have the same name, which you use for query and column name must be same as you use for retrieving values from database.

**Step2:-** Go to Start >control panel >Administrative tool > Data source (ODBC).

**Step3:-** Double click on Data source (ODBC), click on "Add" button, Select MS Access driver...click on "Finish" button.

**Step4:-** Give name to "Data source name". Click on "Select" button and browse your MS access file of ".mdb" extension .Click "OK"

**Step5:-** Now your database is ready to connect using JDBC-ODBC bridge driver. For this you have to mention Data source name in your application.

## 6.2. JDBC Drivers Types

JDBC driver implementations vary because of the wide variety of operating systems and hardware platforms in which Java operates. Sun has divided the implementation types into four categories, Types 1, 2, 3, and 4, which are explained below:

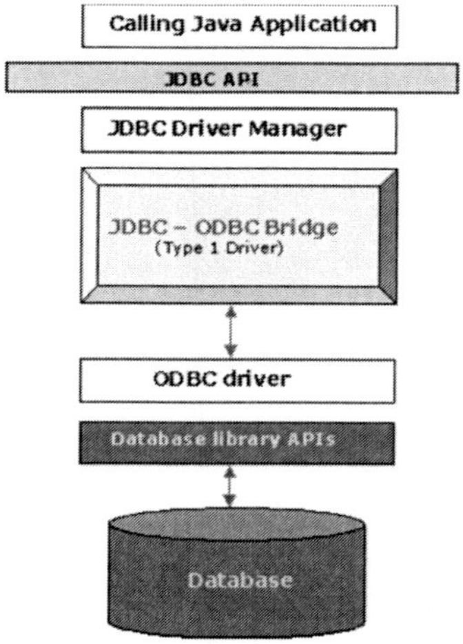


### *Type 1: JDBC-ODBC Bridge Driver*

The JDBC type 1 driver, also known as the JDBC-ODBC bridge, is a database driver implementation that employs the ODBC driver to connect to the database. The driver converts JDBC method calls into ODBC function calls.

### *Advantage*

The JDBC-ODBC Bridge allows access to almost any database, since the database's ODBC drivers are already available.

### *Disadvantages*

1. Since the Bridge driver is not written fully in Java, Type 1 drivers are not portable.
2. A performance issue is seen as a JDBC call goes through the bridge to the ODBC driver, then to the database, and this applies even in the reverse process. They are the slowest of all driver types.
3. The client system requires the ODBC Installation to use the driver.
4. Not good for the Web.

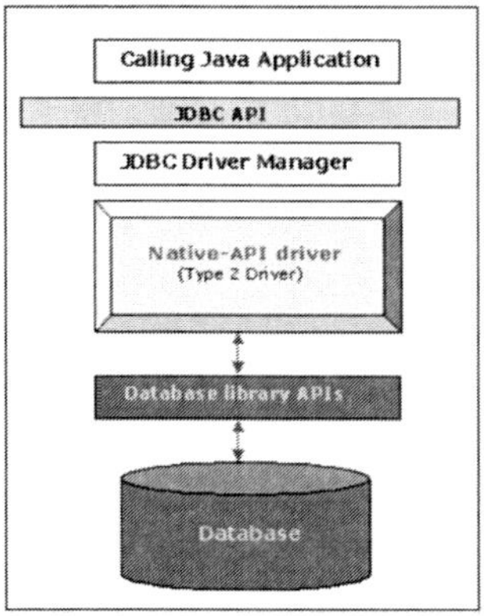


### *Type 2: JDBC-Native API*

The JDBC type 2 driver, also known as the Native-API driver, is a database driver implementation that uses the client-side libraries of the database. The driver converts JDBC method calls into native calls of the database API.

### *Advantage*

The distinctive characteristic of type 2 jdbc drivers are that they are typically offer better performance than the JDBC-ODBC Bridge as the layers of communication (tiers) are less than that of Type 1 and also it uses Native api which is Database specific.

### *Disadvantage*

1. Native API must be installed in the Client System and hence type 2 drivers cannot be used for the Internet.
2. Like Type 1 drivers, it's not written in Java Language which forms a portability issue.
3. If we change the Database we have to change the native api as it is specific to a database.
4. Usually not thread safe.

### *Type 3: JDBC-Net pure Java*

The JDBC type 3 driver, also known as the Pure Java Driver for Database Middleware, is a database driver implementation which makes use of a middle tier between the calling program and the database. The middle-tier (application server) converts JDBC calls directly or indirectly into the vendor-specific database protocol.

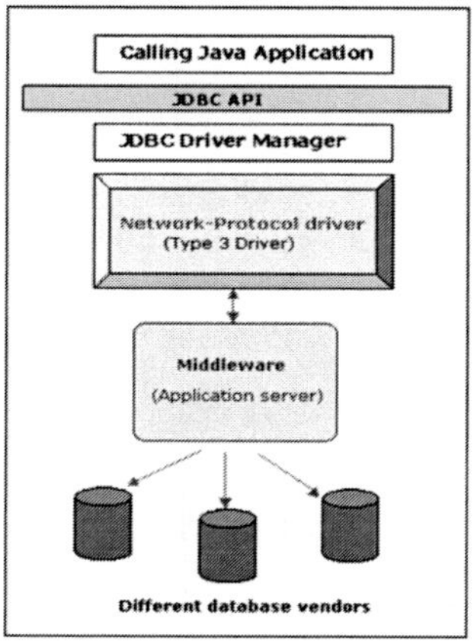


### *Advantage*

1. This driver is server-based, so there is no need for any vendor database library to be present on client machines.
2. This driver is fully written in Java and hence Portable.
3. It is suitable for the web.
4. There are many opportunities to optimize portability, performance, and scalability.
5. The net protocol can be designed to make the client JDBC driver very small and fast to load.
6. The type 3 driver typically provides support for features such as caching (connections, query results, and so on), load balancing, and advanced
   system administration such as logging and auditing.
7. This driver is very flexible allows access to multiple databases using one driver.
8. They are the most efficient amongst all driver types.

### *Disadvantage*

It requires another server application to install and maintain. Traversing the record set may take longer, since the data comes through the backend server.

### *Type 4: JDBC-Native Protocol Driver (Thin)*

The JDBC type 4 driver, also known as the Direct to Database Pure Java Driver, is a database driver implementation that converts JDBC calls directly into a vendor-specific database protocol. Therefore it is called a THIN driver.

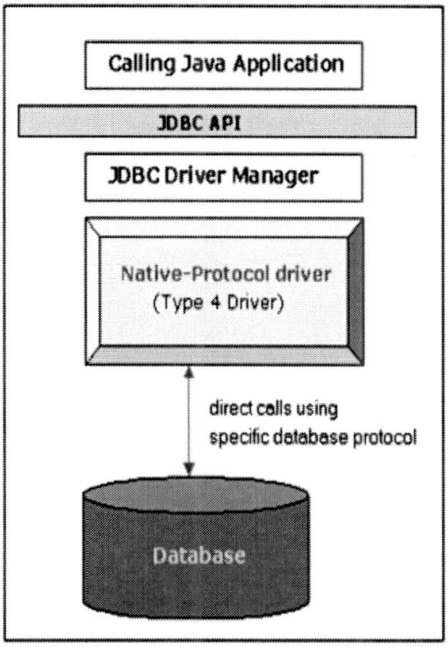


### *Advantage*

1. The major benefit of using type 4 jdbc drivers are that they are completely written in Java to achieve platform independence and eliminate deployment administration issues. It is most suitable for the web.
2. Number of translation layers is very less i.e. type 4 JDBC drivers don't have to translate database requests to ODBC or a native connectivity interface or to pass the request on to another server, performance is typically quite good.
3. You don't need to install special software on the client or server. Further, these drivers can be downloaded dynamically.

### *Disadvantage*

With type 4 drivers, the user needs a different driver for each database.

## 6.3. Package javax.sql

Provides the API for server side data source access and processing from the Java programming language. This package supplements the java.sql package and, as of the version 1.4 releases, is included in the Java2 SDK, Standard Edition. It remains an essential part of the Java 2 SDK, Enterprise Edition (J2EE).

| Interface Summary | |
|---|---|
| **ConnectionEventListener** | An object that registers to be notified of events generated by a PooledConnection object. |
| **ConnectionPoolDataSource** | A factory for PooledConnection objects. |
| **DataSource** | A factory for connections to the physical data source that this DataSource object represents. |
| **PooledConnection** | An object that provides hooks for connection pool management. |
| **RowSet** | The interface that adds support to the JDBC API for the JavaBeans™ component model. |
| **RowSetInternal** | The interface that a RowSet object implements in order to present itself to a RowSetReader or RowSetWriter object. |
| **RowSetListener** | An interface that must be implemented by a component that wants to be notified when a significant event happens in the life of a RowSet object. |
| **RowSetMetaData** | An object that contains information about the columns in a RowSet object. |
| **RowSetReader** | The facility that a disconnected RowSet object calls on to populate itself with rows of data. |
| **RowSetWriter** | An object that implements the RowSetWriter interface, called a *writer*. |
| **XAConnection** | An object that provides support for distributed transactions. |
| **XADataSource** | A factory for XAConnection objects that is used internally. |

| Class Summary | |
|---|---|
| **ConnectionEvent** | An Event object that provides information about the source of a connection-related event. |
| **RowSetEvent** | An Event object generated when an event occurs to a RowSet object. |

The javax.sql package provides for the following:

1. The DataSource interface as an alternative to the DriverManager for establishing a connection with a data source
2. Connection pooling
3. Distributed transactions
4. Rowsets

Applications use the DataSource and RowSet APIs directly, but the connection pooling and distributed transaction APIs are used internally by the middle-tier infrastructure.

### *Using a DataSource Object to Make a Connection*

The javax.sql package provides the preferred way to make a connection with a data source. The DriverManager class, the original mechanism, is still valid, and code using it will continue to run. However, the newer DataSource mechanism is preferred because it offers many advantages over the DriverManager mechanism.

These are the main advantages of using a DataSource object to make a connection:

- Applications do not need to hard code a driver class.
- Changes can be made to a data source's properties, which mean that it is not necessary to make changes in application code when something about the data source or driver changes.
- Connection pooling and distributed transactions are available through a DataSource object that is implemented to work with the middle-tier infrastructure. Connections made through the DriverManager do not have connection pooling or distributed transaction capabilities.

Driver vendors provide DataSource implementations. A particular DataSource object represents a particular physical data source, and each connection the DataSource object creates is a connection to that physical data source.

A logical name for the data source is registered with a naming service that uses the Java Naming and Directory Interface (JNDI) API, usually by a system administrator or someone performing the duties of a system administrator. An application can retrieve the DataSource object it wants by doing a lookup on the logical name that has been registered for it. The application can then use the DataSource object to create a connection to the physical data source it represents.

A DataSource object can be implemented to work with the middle tier infrastructure so that the connections it produces will be pooled for reuse. An application that uses such a DataSource implementation will automatically get a connection that participates in connection pooling.

A DataSource object can also be implemented to work with the middle tier infrastructure so that the connections it produces can be used for distributed transactions without any special coding.

### *Connection Pooling*

Connections made via a DataSource object that is implemented to work with a middle tier connection pool manager will participate in connection pooling. This can improve performance dramatically because creating new connections is very expensive. Connection pooling allows a connection to be used and reused, thus cutting down substantially on the number of new connections that need to be created.

Connection pooling is totally transparent. It is done automatically in the middle tier of a J2EE configuration, so from an application's viewpoint, no change in code is required. An application simply uses the DataSource.getConnection method to get the pooled connection and uses it the same way it uses any Connection object.

The classes and interfaces used for connection pooling are:

- ConnectionPoolDataSource
- PooledConnection
- ConnectionEvent
- ConnectionEventListener

The connection pool manager, a facility in the middle tier of three-tier architecture, uses these classes and interfaces behind the scenes. When a ConnectionPoolDataSource object is called on to create a PooledConnection object, the connection pool manager will register as a ConnectionEventListener object with the new PooledConnection object. When the connection is closed or there is an error, the connection pool manager (being a listener) gets a notification that includes a ConnectionEvent object.

### *Distributed Transactions*

As with pooled connections, connections made via a DataSource object that is implemented to work with the middle tier infrastructure may participate in distributed transactions. This gives an application the ability to involve data sources on multiple servers in a single transaction.

The classes and interfaces used for distributed transactions are:

- XADataSource
- XAConnection

These interfaces are used by the transaction manager; an application does not use them directly.

The XAConnection interface is derived from the PooledConnection interface, so what applies to a pooled connection also applies to a connection that is part of a distributed transaction.

A transaction manager in the middle tier handles everything transparently. The only change in application code is that an application cannot do anything that would interfere with the transaction manager's handling of the transaction. Specifically, an application cannot call the methods Connection.commit orConnection.rollback, and it cannot set the connection to be in auto-commit mode (that is, it cannot call Connection.setAutoCommit(true)).

An application does not need to do anything special to participate in a distributed transaction. It simply creates connections to the data sources it wants to use via the DataSource.getConnection method, just as it normally does. The transaction manager manages the transaction behind the scenes.

The XADataSource interface creates XAConnection objects, and each XAConnection object creates an XAResource object that the transaction manager uses to manage the connection.

***Rowsets***

The RowSet interface works with various other classes and interfaces behind the scenes. These can be grouped into three categories.

1. **Event Notification**
   - **RowSetListener**
     - A RowSet object is a JavaBeans™ component because it has properties and participates in the JavaBeans event notification mechanism. The RowSetListener interface is implemented by a component that wants to be notified about events that occur to a particular RowSet object. Such a component registers itself as a listener with a rowset via the RowSet.AddRowSet Listener method.
     - When the RowSet object changes one of its rows, changes all of it rows, or moves its cursor, it also notifies each listener that is registered with it. The listener reacts by carrying out its implementation of the notification method called on it.
   - **RowSetEvent**
     - As part of its internal notification process, a RowSet object creates an instance of RowSetEvent and passes it to the listener. The listener can use this RowSetEvent object to find out which rowset had the event.

2. **Metadata**

- **RowSetMetaData**
    - This interface, derived from the ResultSetMetaData interface, provides information about the columns in a RowSet object. An application can use RowSetMetaData methods to find out how many columns the rowset contains and what kind of data each column can contain.
    - The RowSetMetaData interface provides methods for setting the information about columns, but an application would not normally use these methods. When an application calls the RowSet method execute, the RowSet object will contain a new set of rows, and its RowSetMetaData object will have been internally updated to contain information about the new columns.

3. **The Reader/Writer Facility**

- A RowSet object that implements the RowSetInternal interface can call on the RowSetReader object associated with it to populate itself with data. It can also call on the RowSetWriter object associated with it to write any changes to its rows back to the data source from which it originally got the rows. A rowset that remains connected to its data source does not need to use a reader and writer because it can simply operate on the data source directly.
- **RowSetInternal**
    - By implementing the RowSetInternal interface, a RowSet object gets access to its internal state and is able to call on its reader and writer. A rowset keeps track of the values in its current rows and of the values that immediately preceded the current ones, referred to as the *original* values. A rowset also keeps track of (1) the parameters that have been set for its command and (2) the connection that was passed to it, if any. A rowset uses the RowSetInternal methods behind the scenes to get access to this information. An application does not normally invoke these methods directly.
- **RowSetReader**
    - A disconnected RowSet object that has implemented the RowSetInternal interface can call on its reader (the RowSetReader object associated with it) to populate it with data. When an application calls the RowSet.execute method that method calls on the rowset's reader to do much of the work. Implementations can vary widely, but generally a reader makes a connection to the data source, reads data from the data source and populates the rowset with it, and closes the connection. A reader

may also update the RowSetMetaData object for its rowset. The rowset's internal state is also updated, either by the reader or directly by the method RowSet execute.

- **RowSetWriter**
    - A disconnected RowSet object that has implemented the RowSetInternal interface can call on its writer (the RowSetWriter object associated with it) to write changes back to the underlying data source. Implementations may vary widely, but generally, a writer will do the following:
    - Make a connection to the data source
    - Check to see whether there is a conflict, that is, whether a value that has been changed in the rowset has also been changed in the data source
    - Write the new values to the data source if there is no conflict
    - Close the connection

The RowSet interface may be implemented in any number of ways, and anyone may write an implementation. Developers are encouraged to use their imaginations in coming up with new ways to use rowsets.

## 6.4. Accessing a Database from a JSP Page

Java cannot talk to a database until it is registered as a data source to your system.

### *Connect a JSP to an MSAccess Database*

We will now describe the Java code required to connect to the database although at this point we will not yet query it. If the program runs successfully, it indicates that the previous registration steps have been successful. We will first give a simplified version of the code.

The JSP program has to do several things:

- Identify the source files for Java to handle SQL.
- Load a software driver program that lets Java connect to the database.
- Execute the driver to establish the connection.

### *The required (simplified) JSP syntax to do this follows:*

```
<%@ page import="java.sql.*" %>
<%
Connection conn=null;
try
{
```

```
        Class.forName ("sun.jdbc.odbc.JdbcOdbcDriver");
        conn = DriverManager.getConnection("jdbc:odbc:Mimi", "", "");
}
catch (Exception exc)
{
        out.println(exc.toString() + "");
}
out.println ("Database Connected.");
conn.close ( );
out.println ("Database closed.");
%>
```

The Class.forName method loads the driver for MS Access. Remember this is Java so the name is case-sensitive. If you misspell or misidentify the data source name, you'll get an error message "Data source name not found and no default driver specified". The DriverManager. getConnection method connects the program to the database identified by the data source Mimi allowing the program to make queries, inserts, selects, etc.

### *Insert Records in Database using JSP*

- Create a Statement object - which has methods for handling SQL.
- Define an SQL query - such as an insert query.
- Execute the query.

```
Statement stm = conn.createStatement ( );
String s = "INSERT INTO Managers VALUES ('Charlie')";
stm.executeUpdate (s);
```

The Connection object conn that was previously created has methods that allow us to in turn create a Statement object. A simple example of a Select is given in testCase012 where a fixed query is defined. The relevant code is:

```
String s = "SELECT * FROM Managers";
ResultSet r = stm.executeQuery(s);
while ( r.next( ) )
{
out.print ("Name: " + r.getString ("name") );
out.println(" Age : " + r.getString ("age" ) );
}
```

## 6.5. Introduction to Struts Framework

The Struts Framework is a standard for developing well-architected Web applications. It has the following features:

- Open source
- Based on the Model-View-Controller (MVC) design paradigm, distinctly separating all three levels:
  - **Model:** application state
  - **View:** presentation of data (JSP, HTML)
  - **Controller:** routing of the application flow
- Implements the JSP Model 2 Architecture
- Stores application routing information and request mapping in a single core file, struts-config.xml

The Struts Framework, itself, only fills in the View and Controller layers. The Model layer is left to the developer.

### *Architecture Overview*

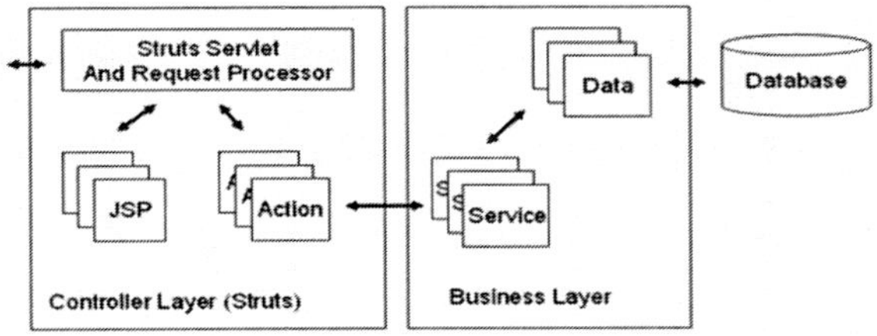


All incoming requests are intercepted by the Struts servlet controller. The Struts Configuration file struts-config.xml is used by the controller to determine the routing of the flow. This flow consists of an alternation between two transitions:

| | |
|---|---|
| **From View to Action** | A user clicks on a link or submits a form on an HTML or JSP page. The controller receives the request, looks up the mapping for this request, and forwards it to an action. The action in turn calls a Model layer (Business layer) service or function. |
| **From Action to View** | After the call to an underlying function or service returns to the action class, the action forwards to a resource in the View layer and a page is displayed in a web browser. |

The diagram below describes the flow in more detail:

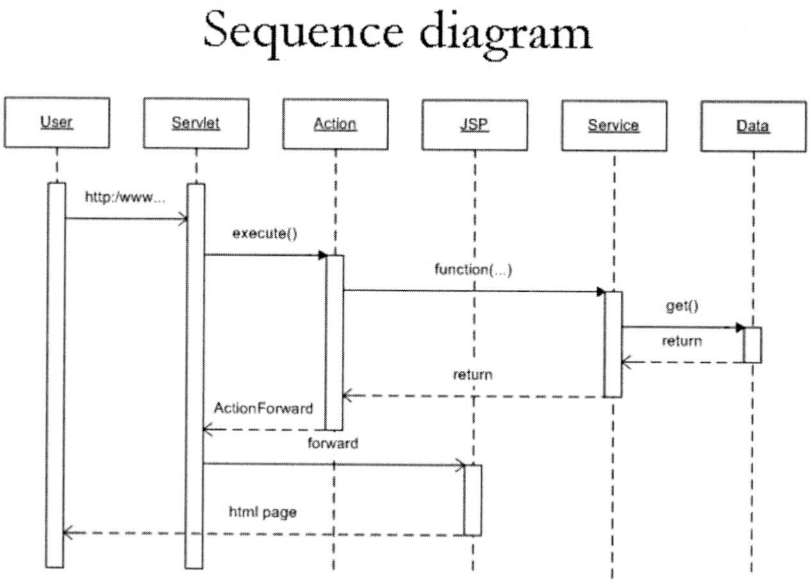


1. **User** clicks on a link in an HTML page.
2. **Servlet** controller receives the request, looks up mapping information in struts-config.xml, and routes to an action.
3. **Action** makes a call to a Model layer service.
4. **Service** makes a call to the Data layer (database) and the requested data is returned.
5. **Service** returns to the action.
6. **Action** forwards to a View resource (JSP page)
7. **Servlet** looks up the mapping for the requested resource and forwards to the appropriate JSP page.
8. **JSP** file is invoked and sent to the browser as HTML.
9. **User** is presented with a new HTML page in a web browser.

## 6.6. Struts Components

### *The Controller*

This receives all incoming requests. Its primary function is the mapping of a request URI to an action class selecting the proper application module. It's provided by the framework.

### *The Struts-Config.xml File*

This file contains all of the routing and configuration information for the Struts application. This XML file needs to be in the WEB-INF directory of the application.

### *Action Classes*

It's the developer's responsibility to create these classes. They act as bridges between user-invoked URIs and business services. Actions process a request and return an Action Forward object that identifies the next component to invoke. They're part of the Controller layer, not the Model layer.

### *View Resources*

View resources consist of Java Server Pages, HTML pages, JavaScript and Stylesheet files, Resource bundles, JavaBeans, and Struts JSP tags.

### *ActionForms*

These greatly simplify user form validation by capturing user data from the HTTP request. They act as a "firewall" between forms (Web pages) and the application (actions). These components allow the validation of user input before proceeding to an Action. If the input is invalid, a page with an error can be displayed.

### *Model Components*

The Struts Framework has no built-in support for the Model layer. Struts support any model components:

* JavaBeans
* EJB
* CORBA
* JDO
* any other